John Henry Mullridge

The Ghost of
Hampton Plantation

John Henry Rutledge

The Ghost of Hampton Plantation

a parable by NANCY RHYNE
as if told by Sue Alston

SANDLAPPER PUBLISHING CO., INC.
ORANGEBURG, SOUTH CAROLINA

Copyright © 1997 Nancy Rhyne

All rights reserved.

Published by Sandlapper Publishing Co., Inc.
Orangeburg, South Carolina 29115

FIRST EDITION

Second Printing, 2004

Photographs by Sid Rhyne

Manufactured in the United States of America

Library of Congress Cataloging-in-Publication Data

Rhyne, Nancy, 1926–
    John Henry Rutledge: the ghost of Hampton Plantation : a parable
/ by Nancy Rhyne ; presented as if told by Sue Alston.
      p.   cm.
    ISBN 0-87844-131-X
    1. Hampton Plantation (S.C.)—History. 2. Plantation life—South
Carolina—Charleston County. 3. Rutledge, John Henry, 1809–1830—
Homes and haunts—South Carolina—Charleston County. 4. Rutledge
family. 5. Alston, Sue, ca. 1873–1983. I. Alston, Sue, ca.
1873–1983. II. Title.
F279.H25R48 1996
975.7'91—dc20   96-42355
                                              CIP

Prologue

According to unofficial records, Sue Alston, a child of emancipated slaves, was born in 1873. On a warm autumn day in 1972 I drove toward Sue's house at Hampton Plantation, on the South Santee River about forty miles north of the city of Charleston, South Carolina. It was to be my first visit with Sue, and I was thinking about her advanced age. Later on, I would learn that she herself didn't know *zackly* how old she was. "If the eye open this February, I might be one [hundred], or one and two, or one and six." She did know that her birthday was February 6 and her wedding anniversary was March 7.

Others who had met Sue suggested what my visit would be like. I could see her cabin before I drove into the yard. She was sitting on the small porch, a colorful kerchief tightly wound around her head, large hoop earrings hanging from her ears, a corncob pipe in her mouth, and a cup of coffee balanced on her knee. She seemed ancient in her appearance.

"Yas!" she fairly screamed. "Come on over here. I tell you what I can't forgot!" Her voice startled me. It resounded like a trumpet. "I tell you 'bout Hampton house," she said of the mansion believed to have been built between 1730 and 1750.

The Hampton Plantation house was of such magnificence and immense dimensions—over 10,000 square feet— that although it was only a few feet above sea level it was thought of as being *on top of the world*.

Before I began my tour with Sue through the legends of Hampton Plantation, I had expected her path to the past to be as crooked as a crab's gait. Instead, it was as straight as a strand line at low tide. I saw moments of Hampton Plantation's greatness flicker.

For the interview, we settled ourselves on her front porch. She talked about manners—suitable behavior and appearance being hallmarks of her philosophy—and the emphasis of the South throughout history on manners and principle. She related a story of honor, entwined with melancholy. Her riveting narrative focused on the ways in which various members of the plantation family tried to cope with the demands of honor and the trials of melancholy.

I visited Sue several times over the next few years. Her story rang out like a battle cry. There was never an instant when I believed she was inaccurate or merely daydreaming. Nothing *came back* to her; it had never left her.

To every prelude there is a postlude. . . .

One day Sue told me she was "waitin' to see when the Lord come a-callin'." He came "a-callin'" for her the first week of December, 1983. The local newspaper published her age as 110. On that day in December, now more than ten years ago, Sue Alston's narrative ended. Through this volume, I'd like to share her story with you.

I call Sue's tale of John Henry Rutledge, the ghost of Hampton Plantation, a parable. Remember, a parable is a story that teaches an essential truth and demands from the listener a response. There are many parables in the Bible. Among them are the good samaritan, the prodigal son, and the book of Jonah. The fact that stories like these are called parables rather than biographies does not detract from the truths they convey.

The predominant characters in this book are real. Although this is a work of nonfiction, it bears mentioning that where the narrative strays from strict nonfiction, my intention has been to remain faithful to the characters and to the essential train of events as they happened. If reality is in any way distorted, it is because I intended to discover, illuminate, or underscore truths that otherwise would have gone unvoiced.

It is my desire that the parable of John Henry Rutledge rage and burn on the pages that follow as it did in Sue Alston's heart.

Nancy Rhyne
Myrtle Beach, SC

dedicated to

two of Charleston's best students,
Terri and Brandon Hair

John Henry Rutledge

The Ghost of Hampton Plantation

*There is no king who has not had
a slave among his ancestors and
no slave who has not had a king
among his.*

Helen Keller
Story of My Life

.

*'Tis far off,
and rather like a dream,
than an assurance
That my remembrance
warrants.*

William Shakespeare
Tempest
Act I. Sc. 1

The First Begin

You wanta hear that old story 'bout John Henry Rutledge—that ghost of Hampton? Oh, Missus, I try my best to scrub his blood off the floor but it just bubble right back up again. I tell you 'bout that man. That I can't forgot. Me old missus, Margaret Hamilton Seabrook Rutledge, Archibald mother, tell me that story. Ev'ry afternoon we sit under the tree or on the porch. I comb her hair, and she tell me the old story. She bring that big old book to the front, and she read and talk 'bout all them people. Them stories I can't forgot.

Missus, you know the Horry—Marse Daniel and Missus Harriott Pinckney Horry, the gran'mother and gran'father of Marse John Henry Rutledge? That was the first begin at Hampton Plantation. Yas, the first begin. That story begin with them. The Horry own Hampton in that day. The only servant they have was Alston. That was the first begin for the Alston too. See zackly how far they come from? That was how it start. But let me tell you somethin' 'bout Hampton. Hampton Plantation was some place in that day and time. I been there. I seen things.

I can't say my feelin' be good all the time now, but they pretty good for someone 'bout to reach the first hundred and start on the second hundred. You know how I used to git up in the mornin', wash me face, think 'bout gittin' on that job at four o'clock in the mornin'? Oh, I ain't got that good feelin' now. But me old feelin', like when I used to talk with me old Missus, oh they was the best feelin' I ever knew. That was the biggest time. Oh, Missus, what can I say? I 'clare to God that was the best time.

When I git up in the mornin', the first thing I did was jump out the bed and thank the Lord for the rest. Then I go to the washer and wash myself. Dress myself. When I was a servant at Hampton Plantation I wear a black dress with a bib and a big sash and a big red handkerchief with the Yankee leaves. Big white apron with sash and bib. I was workin' right there in the house.

When I go to the mansion at four o'clock in the mornin', me old Missus, she was in the pantry. And ev'ry mornin' as I git there, my Missus git that big old beautiful teapot, and she git it full of the old tea leaf, and git me a mug full of hot tea. Yas, ma'am. Now she not git out the good chinas; she git them big old mug. And ev'ry mornin' I finish drink my tea, and I go out to the kitchen. We didn't have the kitchen in the big house. No, not like now'day. We use the outside-the-house kitchen to cook, but in the big house there was the pantry. See? And there always was a big fire in the pantry on cold mornin's.

Oh, man, if I was to tell you the truth this afternoon, Missus, Hampton Plantation was heaven to me, and ever'body else. Missus, they say when they was sellin' people, ever'body was prayin' to go to Hampton Plantation. Want to be Rutledge people! But go to Hampton? No! No! No! Hampton servant be Alston people. Alston people! When the Horry own Hampton, the servant was Alston people. See zackly how it start? See how far the Alston come from? All the way back to the Horry. And the way I look at it, when Marse Daniel choose Missus Harriott Pinckney for his wife, that was the first begin.

Me husband Prince Alston, was Rutledge people. Me? This is how that come 'bout: me great-gran'mother Lydia, a Cherokee Indian woman with all that old long black hair, come from Fairfield Plantation. That was the old Blake place. That was when my people come to Hampton. I was a Colleton, Sue Colleton. I marry Prince Alston in nineteen aught five.

Back in that day and time, ever'thing at Hampton have a name. Them Alston people way back yonder clear the land for the rice fields. That was a task! Clean 'em of all that vine and tree and thing, and smooth 'em out. That be the hardest labor you ever hear

Sue Alston on the front porch of her home, early 1970s.

tell of 'cept when the people in bondage build the pyramids in Egypt. After all fields what border on the river been perfectly clear, they plant rice. Always high price for rice in England. The Horry and Rutledge people way back yonder be millionaire. And ev'ry rice field have a name. Some of them come to my mind now. They was Romney, Montgomery, Smallpox, and Peachtree. The forest been give names. The Pretty Woods was near the mansion, and the Pasture Woods was far away. All swamp been give names. One was Big Mouth; another was Deer Lick.

Daniel Horry, the gran'father of Marse John Henry Rutledge, the ghost, was a millionaire sure 'nough. First wife of Marse Daniel was Missus Judith Serre. Both of them was of the French, you know, what they call the French Huguenot what settle here on the South Santee River. Marse Daniel and Missus Judith have two head of children. Marse Daniel outlive that wife and both children. He was the finest man you ever hear tell of. Tall, handsome a man as you ever lay your eya on. And he own Hampton, Missus. Daniel Horry be the marse of Hampton Plantation.

Don't you know ev'ry head of woman turn to look when he pass by? But Marse Daniel be careful who he pick for a wife. Very careful. Have to have a good missus. He pick just right when he take Missus Harriott Pinckney. You know the Pinckney, Missus? Marse Charles and Missus Eliza? They teach Missus Harriott manners, sure 'nough. If you not have a nickel in your pocket you can have manners, and she sure had that.

In a few years Missus Harriott fancy rest on Marse Daniel. That come as no surprise. Ev'ry year some big rice plantin' fam'lies be unite by marriage. Marse Daniel, as he was the only son, was a very wealthy man, ownin' many plantation along the Santee River. But Hampton was the biggest jewel in the string.

Weddin' plans was arrange, and that weddin' take place on the fifteenth day of February, 1768. You know, Missus, when a woman marry a planter, certain furniture go with the bridals. Each bride git a lofty mahogany four-poster bed with tester, canopy, curtain, and valance, complete. The post—what might from height and size be call pillars—all was carve with the rice stalk, the heavy clusterin' ear showin' as plain as can be. To climb into one of them bed the bride have to mount a set of carpet steps. Missus Harriott bed still be in existence, but only the Lord know where.

To tell you the truth, Missus, I bring my mind back to them days when me old missus bring out the big old book. We sit on the porch, and she read it to me. I can't forgot what she read 'bout Missus Harriott and Marse Daniel. He study law at London Inner Temple and been call to the English bar. And he own Hampton, Missus. For sure he own that.

Missus Harriott speak French and could hold forth on any topic from religion to politics. Her disposition was as calm as the sea. She have manners and principle. And she always write she letters two time, like her mother taught her. Missus Eliza write the letter what she plan to send away, and then she write it again all the way down and she put that second letter in her letter box. Missus Harriott know how to do that. Me old Missus sometime bring out that old letter box to the porch and read to me from them letters, and that I can't forgot.

Marse Daniel and Missus Harriott own a fine home down in Chas'n, at the corner of Broad and Legare. And Missus Eliza have that fine home on East Bay what overlook the Cooper River. Missus Harriott and Missus Eliza be mother and daughter, but they also be same as best friend. They didn't stint with their time as they direct a English gardener to keep ever'thing in back of their houses in perfect order.

Inside Missus Harriott Chas'n house, them servant include a housekeeper and her assistant, butler, and footmen. Missus Harriott maid also was a seamster and clearstarcher. The cook have a girl in trainin' and a boy scullion to help her, and there was many laundresses. Marse Daniel have a body servant, and there be a coachman and as many groom and stable boy as Marse Daniel horses demand. It was a gran' fam'ly, and I tell you that this mornin'.

When Missus Eliza write to her friend in England, Missus Boddicotte, she tell 'bout how nobody in them household eat the bread of idleness. No sirree. They not eat that, sure 'nough.

Yas, ma'am, when Marse Daniel Horry pick Missus Harriott for to be the mistress of Hampton Plantation, he pick the perfect wife. Missus Harriott have manners and principle. Oh, she have that all right. And she was a pretty woman, but not a picture of beauty like her mother.

Yas, ma'am, I can't forgot what I hear 'bout Missus Harriott. You want to hear 'bout all of that? Then travel 'long the years with me from that day and time 'til I come to sittin' right here in this chair. It'll take a powerful sight of that pencil to put it all down.

The old people say Missus Harriott fill her carriage with sugar, tea, sweet potato, and thing and take to the sick and old people. She had a good heritage, but mostly she had manners and principle. That was the kind of folk Hampton Plantation sprung from.

You know, Missus, death come in and make alteration, and hard livin' make contrivance, but that time when Missus Harriott and Marse Daniel live at Hampton musta been the best time.

He Paweth in the Valley

I remember hearin' 'bout the horse races in Chas'n. Them men of by-gone days love the turf! All them planter take their thorough-breds down to The New Market Race Course, sometime call Strickland's, whilst it was run by a gentleman of that name. The planter run their horses 'gainst each other. And, Missus, that be a day to remember. When Missus Harriott brother, Marse Charles Cotesworth Pinckney, come home from England, he be part owner of that Chas'n racetrack. Marse Charles and Marse Daniel have the time of their life a-racin' their thoroughbreds on that course.

Missus Harriott was plenty fine, but she not have all that tact her mother have. Missus Eliza, when she git vex with her husband 'bout somethin', keep quiet and not raise a storm. But when Marse Daniel build that racetrack at the inland entrance to Hampton house for to race his thoroughbred horse, Missus Harriott point out to him the best place for the track ain't close to the mansion.

Of course, the main entrance to the mansion been on the river side in that day and time, and that was where the porch with the big old white columns stand. Most visitor who traffic to Hampton come by boat, and Marse Daniel see nothin' wrong with buildin' his race-track at the back of the house, what is the main entrance to Hampton house today.

Missus, when you arrive at Hampton and see that big white mansion with the pillar porch a-gleamin' in the distance, that not be the side of the house where visitors 'rive in them colonial time. No sirree. That sweepin' lawn with them big oak tree what you see today once be Marse Daniel race course.

Marse Daniel and Missus Harriott have some up and down 'bout that racetrack, and Marse Daniel tell her about Marse Fenwick three-and-a-half-mile race course near his mansion on Johns Island. Marse Fenwick raise fine horseflesh, and Marse Daniel always admire the thoroughbred what come from Fenwick Hall.

Missus, can you pretend? You know how to do that? Yas? Zat so? All right. Sue show it to you. Just pretend you see it all with them two eyas. I know all 'bout that horse racin'. Me old Missus bring the big old book to the porch, and she read to me and talk to me, and she tell me all 'bout race day in Chas'n. She recollect 'bout that very well. She used to say, "Who is there, with soul so dead," and then she go right back and tell it like it was happenin' at that very minute. She tell it to me, Missus, and now I tell it you, and you see it too.

Just like that old Jockey Club over the ocean in Paris, where the Prince of Orleans and Marse Charles Lafitte race their best 'flesh,

Hampton Plantation mansion

the New Market and the Jockey Club in Chas'n be fine ones. Yas, indeed.

You still pretending, Missus? All right. We be at the New Market course right now. Just look over yonder. See that? See Marse Ravenel all dress up? His favorite race rider be on Spotless, a bay horse. And look next to him. That's Marse Frank Huger. His rider is 'bout to mount Abdallah. You wonder who that is a-comin' over to talk with them? That's Marse William Henry Drayton, and he a-puttin' on a brag 'bout his horse Shadow. He have along another horse, Adolphus, what been bred by old Brutus. And Brilliant Mare be bred by Marse Edward Fenwick thoroughbred, and that is a horse on its feet—have some pedigree!

Oh them planter be mighty proud of their thoroughbred. Look at them over there. They just like boys again.

Yas, Missus, them was as fine a men as you ever lay your eyas on—a long line of blooded ancestry. And the same go for the horseflesh. They be as good as them horse in Egypt in the time of King Solomon who had all them fine trotter and pacer. Now, Solomon was fond of horses, but he been a wise prince. He know 'bout ever'thing. Yet, Pharaoh not consent for his finest horses to go out of his kingdom, not even to his son-in-law Solomon, without a great tribute. Know what that tribute was? No? It was one hundred and fifty shekel of silver. What a shekel amount to? A shekel be 'bout two shilling and four pence halfpenny, English money.

I wonder what old King Solomon would think 'bout this race you a-witnessin' right now. Solomon with his 40,000 stall of horses for his chariots, and 12,000 horsemen. You know what a horse bring, 'bout the time we a-watchin' this race, here at Hampton Plantation? 'Bout fifteen hundred dollar. But very fast trotter bring twice that— that I know! That I can't forgot.

Oh, Missus, they be fine specimen—as fine as them Job talk about in the Bible. I know the Bible. Can't fool old Sue 'bout stripture. You remember Job said, "He has give the horse stren'th;

he paweth in the valley, and rejoice in his stren'th!" He say that.

Watch now, Missus! You still with Sue?

Race week in Chas'n be some day and time, I tell you right now in the mornin'. The court of justice be adjourn. All school be let out as the hour for startin' the horses draw near. All them store on King Street be close. Business be suspend.

And the people who come just to look at the race, they be turn out in fine feather. They 'rive in splendid equipages with liveried outriders. Men a-wearin' buckskin breeches and top boots. And the ladies, oh, goodness gracious, they ride in carriages pull by four matchin' bay horse, and they be turn out in clothes and jewels from Paris. The prize for this race? Pieces of silver—cup, bowl, or salver—costin' no more than one hundred pound sterlin'. Ev'ry plantation sideboard must have a prize! The big silver bowl on Hampton sideboard was engrave to say MARSE HORRY FILLY WIN OVER MARSE HARLESTON COLT, AT NEW MARKET COURSE. That I can't forgot. Me old Missus tell me all 'bout the race in Chas'n, and I take it in.

It is about time now, Missus. Comin' up. Oh, there go the order to mount. Riders up. Horses have itchin' feet, a-playin' and a-rompin' 'round. That race course is straight, not a slant of a hill in sight. And, Missus, see how quiet it is? You could hear the breast feather of a turkey fall. Yas sirree. Quietness prevail.

Now we watch, Missus. The world drop away and we wait in silence, a-holdin' our breath. There go the word. They off—on the run now, all together. Centinel be fallin' back while Babraham keepin' close up. They a-goin' along now at a tellin' pace, head erec', neck arch, eyas a-flashin'. Oh, Missus, Adolphus takin' the lead. Centinel more than half a distance behind.

Still quiet. See how quiet ever'thing is? Noble keepin' pace at a steady pull, but Coughing Polly and Minuet closin' upon him. Now, look. Minuet makin' a play for the rally home. He still have somethin' left in him. There is a heap of struggle for the pole at the last turn. Minuet fly by and pass the post. *Oh-h-h-h-h!* Marse Daniel

Minuet done won by half a neck, and the others droppin' in the distance. A very close race! Thousands shoutin'. Ever'one around Minuet. A sea of human bein's. They saw it all. Oh, Missus, we been there. We saw it.

I never forgit all that me old Missus tell me 'bout them horses. I see 'em many time in my dream. The thoroughbred was the noblest animal ever 'propriate for the use of man. Missus tell me that racin' render a very important service to the country. It benefit the agriculture interest on ev'ry plantation where there was a taste for fine horseflesh. The horse races was hard work and a passion. And them animal! Oh, how they perform a task for their marse. No one know the pride the marse have if his horse win the race. Pride just bubble up like the blood of John Henry Rutledge, the ghost, after his death.

I tell you, on the last day of racin' durin' that February week when Chas'n races be held, there is a great ball. All marse and missus attend that. Ev'ry year Missus Harriott have a polonaise dress made by the most celebrate dressmaker in Chas'n for that event.

After the race ball, Missus Harriott give a ball at her Chas'n mansion. It is one to remember. She write out the list of what she need for that ball two time, just like her letters. And she give one list to the head cook. The list say fourteen doz plate, fourteen doz knife, fifteen doz fork, nineteen doz spoon, ten doz quart oyster, and four preserve of fowl all perfectly clean and season.

Whilst the cooks work in the outside-the-house kitchen, they pitch a song, same as we cooks here at Hampton. We pitch *I Wanta Go Home*. That song go like this: "There's no rain to wet you. Oh yas, I wanta go home. There's no sun to burn you. Oh yas, I wanta go home. There's no whips a-crackin'. Oh yas, I wanta go home. There's no hard trials. Oh yas, I wanta go home. There's no brother on the wayside. Oh yas, I wanta go home."

The cooks wear long skirt and apron. Scarf 'round their head. They all work and talk and sing at the same time, but certain cooks work with the fowl, and others make the cakes, and like that. They know what was expect of them and they git all the 'gredients they need. No expense was spare.

Scipio was a man what help with the preserve of fowl. That was a masterpiece, sure 'nough. He sing while he clean a small dove, and he slip a strip of bacon inside the dove. Then he take the dove and push it into a partridge. The partridge be slip inside a guinea hen, and the guinea hen go into a wild duck. The duck be place in a capon, and the capon take its place in a goose. The goose go into a turkey. But two of the preserve of fowl end with a peacock. So there be two of turkey and two of peacock. All of that be roast and when it was put on the table, Scipio take a heavy silver knife and slice it down two ways, east and west, and north and south, top to bottom. Then each plate was pile high. He slice 'cross the top, givin' the guest a fourth of a slice or two fourth, or whatever they ask for. There was plenty of the old Madeira wine what been a-ripenin up in the garret. And plenty of coffee.

Missus Harriott serve the old syllabub. I can't forgot that receipt what been hand down to all the Rutledge. They have that old syllabub churn. To one pint of cream add a gill of white wine, the grated rind of one lemon, the white of three egg, and four tablespoon powder sugar. Churn all 'til stiff and turn into crystal cups.

After all the people—them what sit at the damask tablecloth and them what walk 'bout the mansion—be stuff as tight as the preserve of fowl, a band of three slave men git ready for to play fife, drum, and fiddle. After they git warm up, all the men and women join in a country dance. The ball last near all night.

That tell you somethin', Missus, 'bout the social life of Missus Harriott and Marse Daniel. There never be anything like it. Never before nor since.

Blessed are the Children

Missus Harriott be a perfect angel if ever there was one on this earth. 'Member the Good Samaritan? Missus Harriott do all of that and more. Ask any of them old Horry or Rutledge people, and they tell you what a fine woman she was.

Well, now that Marse Daniel and Missus Harriott have their position 'mong the planter society, Missus Harriott feel the next natural step is to have some head of children. She have a good teacher in Missus Eliza and she know plenty 'bout the proper pathway to teach her children to take in their life.

In that day and time, Missus, little girl babies was groom from the cradle up to become mistress of great plantation, to oversee the mansion and direct a large staff of servant. And the boy babies? Planters believe in the first-born right of inheritin'. That boy inherit all the fam'ly property. When any other boy baby come 'long, he got to make his own livin'. And girl baby? She have to marry a planter and git her own plantation that way.

Now, Missus, you understand that old setup, that old Chas'n peckin' order where the first boy be the planter and the inheritor? The next boy and the next and the next be somebody in the profession, like a doctor or lawyer, or tradesman. Nobody in Chas'n look down on any son of a planter what not own the plantation. They all know that privilege go only to the firstborn. But they look down on anyone who not come from the landed gentry.

And that bring on another old peckin' order. You know, the highest of the Chas'n society be the rice planter. And the next be the sea island cotton planter, because that product be mighty nigh as important as rice. And number three be the inland planter, who grow cotton back in the red clay country. And the next be professions, and last come the tradesmen. Some of them tradesmen be blockade runners, you know, like Marse Clark Gable in that movie *Gone with the Wind*.

Oh, yas, Missus, I go down to Chas'n to see that picture show, because Marse Clark Gable come to Hampton Plantation and play his mouth organ on the porch. He was a blockade runner in that old picture show, and bein' a blockade runner was a fine job. Nobody look down on that profession. That be a tradesman, what be call yeoman. Me old Missus tell me all 'bout that. That I can't forgot.

Marse Daniel hope with all his heart to have a boy baby what be the heir to Hampton Plantation. Missus Harriott hope with all her heart to have a girl baby what be the same kind of lady she herself was. And that girl baby must grow up to marry a wealthy rice planter and have her very own plantation to run, just like the boy baby who would inherit Hampton.

Well, Missus, on the thirteenth day of August, 1769, a boy baby be drop by Missus Harriott. He be name Daniel, just like his father. Thirteen day later he been baptize at St. Michael Church in Chas'n. Just over a year go by and that girl baby what be hope for been born. And she be name Harriott like her mother. Them two head of children have plenty of godparents.

Missus Harriott say it be a honor and privilege by the mercy of the Lord to have them babies, and she start their training right away. She teach them children manners and principle. I tell you from the heart Hampton Plantation was some place in that day and time. Good times! Thanks be to the Lord for the good times at Hampton this old head hear 'bout.

But, nothin' ever stay the same. There be drawbacks to ever'thing. It seem there always be someone a-stirrin' up a war, and them English people, what Missus Harriott and Marse Daniel be so fond of, be the ones a-doin' the stirrin'. Marse Daniel be one hundred percent American—woof, warp, and fillin'. And he not like all that funny stuff goin' on in England. Let me tell you what that be 'bout, Missus.

In December of 1773 the East Indian Company ship 257 chest of tea to Chas'n. There was some up and down 'bout what to do 'bout that tea. Some say they should 'spose of the tea and not pay that tax to England. The citizens gather and they decide not to receive that shipment of tea. But they be surprise when they hear tell that customs officers done move the tea off the ship and into the Exchange warehouse.

Think 'bout that, Missus. There was all that old tea leaf, somethin' ever'body love so much, and it be the object of all that fussin'. The doors to that warehouse be lock tight, let me tell you.

South Carolina musta been the only colony to keep the tea. Philadelphia and New York send their load back to England. And Boston? Oh, man! They dump their tea in the harbor. But South Carolina hold on to that old tea leaf and sell it to git money so they can pay for the war 'gainst England they believe was a-comin'.

After that tea dispute, Marse John Rutledge, a Chas'n lawyer, make a pleasin' speech to the town. Marse John was a silver-tongue man, and that be for sure. He have a fine education, first by a tutor and then at the Temple in London. That speech make a impression on the multitude in South Carolina, and all say they believe Marse John have the greatest talent in speakin' of anybody in the colonies. He could sure 'nough shake thing up when he speak.

Marse John Rutledge also be known for his Chas'n wine cellar. He keep two pipe of the famous *Butler 16* Madeira, 'long with port, Lisbon, schnapps, sauterne, ale, demijohn of French brandy, rum, and Irish whiskey. Marse John hisself put away two quart of Madeira daily. He was right proud of that 'complishment.

Durin' that pesky time with England, Missus Harriott brother, Marse Charles Cotesworth Pinckney, marry seventeen-year-old Sally Middleton, daughter of Henry Middleton of Chas'n. He be one of the biggest planter of them day and time, and he start the Middleton Gardens what be known over the world for it beauty. Them big planters like nothin' better than to unite their fam'lies. That keep all the land *under one roof.*

On some 'casions, cousins marry cousins for that purpose.

Blood be strong, and fam'lies be close. Don't you know Missus Harriott call that to the 'tention of her daughter, young Missus Harriott? She tell her to start thinkin' 'bout some planter for to marry at the 'propriate time.

'Though the *quality* could not stop the trouble what be a-brewin' in England, they not allow that to hinder their social life. They still have their banquets and balls. And Marse Daniel still go to Chas'n to race his thoroughbred.

After George III begin havin' rows with the colonies, and he declare that anyone who not agree with him is a traitor and a scoundrel, the colonists start to worry 'bout war and they organize regiments. Officers was chose by ballot cast. In the rankin' of captains, Daniel Horry was sixth. Both Missus Harriott brother, Marse Thomas and Marse Charles Cotesworth, was captains. You see how all this affect Missus Harriott, with her brothers and husband gone off to fight? But she be a woman on her feet, even in war time. She turn Hampton into a sanctuary for women and children.

There was a lot to do, and iffen they like to read, Hampton Plantation had one of the finest library in the country. Marse Daniel had sign his books and somebody in the fam'ly have them books even today. Books in the Hampton library include a old book by Sir Edward Coke, *Laws of England*, printed in 1590. Books by authors with names not easy to say was in the library. Florence Nightingale had autograph her book what be there, and some of the most in-use books was by Tennyson, Dickens, and . . . oh, I can't remember all of them writer, Missus.

Marse Daniel not git along well in that war. The enemy seize him, but he finally git his parole. Then somethin' else bad happen. Marse Daniel, active 'gainst the British from the beginnin', make a controversial choice. When he hear that a company of the enemy was 'bout to enter the Hampton area of the Santee River, he desert the Patriot cause for fear that Missus Harriott and his children face harm.

Marse Thomas write to his sister, Missus Harriott, and he say how disappointed he is 'bout his brother-in-law decision.

Missus Harriott turn her 'tention to her children. She decide then and there, war or no war, she was gone send her son to England for his education. She wrote General Nathanael Greene several letters—always writin' each letter twice and puttin' a copy in the letter box—askin' permission to send rice from Hampton to England to pay for her son education there. Missus Harriott know a schooner stash with Carolina rice go a long way on payin' for a English education! Marse Daniel settle on goin' to England with his son.

Now, Missus, you can understand why that move not make Marse Daniel very popular in South Carolina. Goin' to England durin' that war didn't seem to be the thing to do. But after he take his son over there, he turn right 'round and come home. But what do you think? He be detain in Chas'n. All his fam'ly was mighty upset and letters go a-flyin'. Missus Harriott put pen to paper, pleadin' her husband case. Sad letters!

But Missus Harriott never let anything git her down. She did not kick up a fuss. She still be the good-taste, good-manners hostess, and she show her daughter Harriott how to be the same. That daughter was bein' groom to marry a planter and Missus Harriott know she have to keep up that trainin', no matter what.

When the old Swamp Fox, General Francis Marion, was fightin' closeby, he stop in at Hampton and tell Missus Harriott to *take protection, make provision, keep up communication, and send information to the men in camp.* Missus Harriott fill him to the brim with any news she had obtain. Before he take his leave, she give him some good wine and a hearty meal. The general make Hampton a regular stoppin' place.

One day the old Swamp Fox be a-restin' in one of Missus Harriott chairs, sippin' wine and talkin' with Missus Harriott. The general been in a battle and he was 'bout wore out. He nod off.

Missus Harriott and her daughter and the general be alone in the house. Just then the women hear the sound of hoofs in the yard. Then they hear a voice, and the general wake up real quick and say, "That be Colonel Banastre Tarleton, my archenemy. Get me outa here."

Missus Harriott point to a little door what lead to a secret passageway. The general jump up so fast he break off a arm of the Chippendale wing chair where he was a-restin'. He race through the secret passage, jump on his horse, and fairly fly to Wambaw Creek. He cross that and make haste for Hampton Island and on to South Santee River.

As I think 'bout it now, I can almost see him, a-swimmin' his horse 'cross that river to the safety of the delta he know so well. That was why they call him the Swamp Fox. In the swamp no enemy could catch him.

And you know what Missus Harriott do? Just as brave and courageous as any soldier who fight in a war, she go right to the front door and open it to Colonel Tarleton, a devil standin' there in the shape of a man. His piercin' blue eyas look her over.

"Why, Colonel Tarleton," Missus Harriott say graciouslike, "you must be exhausted. Come in and have a nice supper with me."

Now Missus Harriott had prepare that good supper for the old Swamp Fox—'course he didn't have time to eat it. Colonel Tarleton 'cept her invitation and enter the house. He enjoy his supper very much and then ask to see the library. Missus Harriott show him the books and point out the most valuable ones. He look 'round, and he go on and on 'bout the books. . . . Missus Harriott write in her journal that his voice remind her of a organ with many stops.

After awhile, the Colonel thank her for her hospitality and leave. She go back to the library to straighten up, and what do you think? Tarleton had stole the fine volume of Milton—a Baskerville edition, they say, in crimson and gold. Many year later someone find that same volume in a London bookstall and return it to Hampton Plantation.

Little Missus Harriott tell that story 'bout her mother, and General Marion breakin' off the arm of that Chippendale, with the greatest delight. She remember all the detail for all of her life.

The British was defeat on the nineteenth day of October, 1781, and that war been the longest war what ever been fight on American soil. General Peter Horry was a famous man in that war. He was Marse Daniel cousin, and he also be General Marion senior right-hand man. When he come to Hampton, he now and then rap out a oath, but Missus Harriott not open her mouth. When any other man in that house, such as Marse Charles Cotesworth Pinckney, Missus Harriott brother, rap out a oath, Missus Harriott say, "Charles, Charles, you forgit . . . the girls," meanin' little Missus Harriott and her cousins who spent most of their time at Hampton. The talk would sure 'nough be clean up right away. But when "Cousin Peter" let out a ugly word, she look down and say nothin'. If the girls bridle, she say, "Peter can swear when and where he choose."

Missus Harriott let "Cousin Peter" get by with what she did not approve of, but she never let up in teachin' her only daughter manners and principle. Ever'body at Hampton have to have that. They wouldn'ta had no-manners people nowhere on the place. She tell her daughter how she must marry a planter and teach her children to marry planters or daughters of planters. She make no mistake 'bout that. The daughter learn that lesson very well, but what did it bring her down to? Oh, Missus, sometime I have to sit down in the night and think 'bout the brokenheart day what that old lesson finally bring them down to.

Hands Across and Down the Middle

Marse Daniel be kinda down and out—still a-frettin' about people bein' standoffish. A treaty of peace been sign in London and the American army be disband by the commander in chief, General George Washington. And yet some of them planters not have forgiveness in their heart for Marse Daniel. They think back 'bout Marse Daniel takin' his son to England for his education, and they believe that Marse Daniel show his loyalty to that old country.

You know what the Bible say 'bout forgiveness? That be the basis of God nature, His grace. You know how we pray? "Forgive us our trespass as we forgive them what trespass 'gainst us." Yet, some of them planters be unable to forgive Marse Daniel.

Finally, Marse Daniel give all his energy to church work and try to forgot about them other planters. Marse Daniel believe the only route to heaven be by way of the 'Piscopal Church and he be 'Piscopalian through and through.

But the 'Piscopal Church be languishin' after the war. The old patronage under the royal government been withdrawed and them old churches be shaky, 'cept for them two mighty ones in Chas'n: St. Michael and St. Philip. They flourish same as before war.

And Missus Harriott? What she been doin'? She be a-runnin' her household just the same as always. That year she send Savage, Bird and Savage in England a hundred tierces of rice to pay for a coach of luxury. And when that coach come she just sit right in there and ride on them Chas'n streets like she was the Princess of Wales.

And little Missus Harriott? She fetch out her dolls and talk a whole lot of child/mother talk. She have two dolls, name Dorcas and Priscilla. They was porcelain. She fetch out them dolls and have a big old time. She didn't mince 'round over them dolls. When she find out company was a-comin', she tell the dolls she have invite somebody over to play with them.

After that period of nervous strain, what been goin' on durin' the war, was over, the Low Country begin to have some merriment again. And the sport of horse racin' soon be revive. Them stables what been broke up by the war, and the thoroughbreds what been use for troopers, be call back to duty. But them thoroughbreds been reduce in number, as one of Colonel Tarleton first stunts was to capture four hundred horses—and he ordered, "sixty famous ones." When racin' start up again, there was some new names on the turf, for the middle country now enter the sport of the Low Country gentry.

When the Jockey Club open back up, the Washington Race Course was set up for the comfort of all class. The lady stand mighta been call *modern* with its salon and the fancy retirin' and refreshment rooms. There was the Grand Stand, and a Citizens' Stand open to all. Guests was provide with tickets.

The Washington Course appear merrier than the New Market ever been. There be the same fine animals and the same gentlemen in the glossy top boots and white buckskin breeches. But the use of coaches had now become general. There was some in earlier days but not so many. Even Missus Harriott had her shiny new one there.

Oh, Missus, let's go there now. Me old Missus taught me how to *be there*. You with me?

The horses is paradin' in the enclosure by the startin' post, displayin' their elastic step. Next come the weighin' of the riders, unbucklin' of straps and surcingles. Blankets cover the loins and croup of the animals so as not to unsettle a hair of their glossy coat. And, oh, them grooms and jockeys is a-fired up, a-tinglin', and a-twitterin'. We there. Oh, yas.

Missus, did I tell you 'bout the little fellow who always ride the mare name Rocksanna? No? Just before this one race, the boy fall ill. He recover before race day, but was left with one foot puffed and weak. His marse was General McPherson. The general was a prominent figure on the turf in South Carolina. Credit was due him for improvin' the stock of horses in the state, and maintainin' the manners and principle of racin', what made the Carolina Jockey Club famous. That marse also be the one who turn 'round the sport to gentlemen and keep out the gamblers.

Marse McPherson resolve the boy not be well enough to ride on race day. But the jockey plead, protestin' that the mare would not win with another rider. The master yield and the race begin.

Now, on that jockey foot what been swell, the pressure of the stirrup come to bear. To relieve the pain, the boy throw his weight to the other side. But he done too much and the leather snap! Before the stirrup could fall, the boy catch it, stick it in his teeth, and bring Rocksanna home. Oh, man! He done won that race.

General McPherson allow that boy to carry the trophy, what was a large bowl with racehorses emboss 'round the outside.

In that day and time the cock of the walk horse was Comet, own by Colonel William Alston of Waccamaw. He was the man what the planters call "King Billy," due to his wealth and prestige, and he was the head man in horse racin'.

A race come up at New Market Course when ever'body believe Ranger, Colonel William Washington thoroughbred, would beat Comet. Oh, Missus, that was a race to be reckon with. When Comet, carryin' 140 pounds over the course, beat Ranger, that was the sportin'est affair what ever take place in the South Carolina Low Country.

After the race come the big celebration ball, and after that the fam'ly balls. A ball was not so troublesome a matter, as the large number of well-train servant make things easy. Rugs and carpets was roll back and remove, and the floors rub with beeswax to a bright polish. Chandeliers with their long, glitterin' drops and the girandoles on the little convex mirrors was fill with wax candles. Nosegays was place in the china and cut-glass jars. The panel walls, carve woodwork, cove ceilin's, mirrors in gilt frames, and portraits needed no embellishin'.

All ages went to the balls and dance the minuet and a country dance. At one ball just after the war, General Moultrie, in full regalia, dance the minuet with a lady of suitable age he soon after marry. I would say *that* spin 'round the floor was a stately one.

Nothin' was stately 'bout the country dance. Gran'fathers dance with gran'children, and mothers with their sons. When the slave fiddlers strike up *Hands Across and Down the Middle*, young and old join in, all as happy as children.

Oh, them folk have manners, Missus, and in some regard the manners be right formal. Them chaperone over there on the side, all a-sittin' in a row, lookin' like a Roman Senate, woulda surely spook some of them children.

Supper was somethin' to feast your two eyas on as well as your appetite. Bone turkeys, game, terrapin stew—some call it cooter stew—jellies, creams, custards, and cakes of all kind was all made right there in the house. Then, o' course, there was the Madeira what been a-ripenin' in the cedar-shingle garret.

Yas, Missus, them horse races be some day and time. And you been there, with Sue.

But even with all that gaiety there still was plenty of work to be done at Hampton Plantation.

The Lord Come A-Calling

Missus Sally Middleton Pinckney, the wife of Missus Harriott brother Charles Cotesworth Pinckney, come down with tuberculosis. She been ill a long time. After the Lord come a-callin' for her in 1784, Marse Charles Cotesworth take his three head of children, Missus Maria Henrietta, Missus Harriott, and Missus Eliza Lucas, to Hampton to be with Missus Harriott and Marse Daniel and their daughter Harriott. By that time, Missus Eliza Lucas Pinckney, Missus Harriott mother, be a widow and a-spendin' most of her time at Hampton. So them three little children be a-livin' with their aunt and their gran'mother. You got that, Missus? Little Missus Harriott have a big old time with all that company in the house.

Now listen to me, Missus. You listening? In November of 1785 the Lord come a-callin' for Marse Daniel. He die of liver failure and bilious fever. You see what that mean? Remember what I say 'bout that old system of first-born inheritin'? Oldest son git all the property. That's right. Now you got it.

Young Marse Daniel was sixteen year old and still in Europe! Not only that, but that boy had change his name to Charles Lucas Pinckney Horry! He was said to have 'straordinary quick parts, but he also be idle and willful. Anything he want to do, he just wade in without caution. But glory be to the Almighty that will of Marse Daniel also state that Missus Harriott have the use of Hampton Plantation for her lifetime. And she and her widow mother, Missus Eliza, and her daughter make good use of it.

Long 'bout that time, that son over in Europe go and shake hands for life with a woman with the longest name you ever hear tell of in your life: Missus Elenore Marie Florimonde de Fay La Tour Marbourg. She was a niece of the Marquis de Lafayette. Yas sirree. They have a mighty jolly weddin' of it over there in France. Missus Eliza and Missus Harriott be all aglow over that weddin', 'cause that missus be almost the same as royalty. They talk 'bout the son who not come back to South Carolina, and they reconcile to that.

You see, Missus, sometime the education of planter sons be hurtful to such of them as be destine to follow their father line of work. They return from distant countries with 'pinions and habits what not suit their future prospects. That foreign education what make them better scholars gen'rally make them worse planters. Missus Harriott and her mother realize that and just hope young Marse Daniel fare well in France.

The bride and groom send the fam'ly mirrors and other household items from France, and Missus Eliza and Missus Harriott hang them on the wall. Them two women run Hampton just like it belong to them. And little Missus Harriott, she have three cousin for company.

Six women in that mansion, and they keep up with all the Chas'n society the same as in time past. They go down for the races and balls, and they attend the St. Cecilia Society concerts. That society begin in 1737 with a concert give upon a Thursday what also was St. Cecilia Day. Since that time, it be the most 'lustrious one in all Chas'n society.

When Marse Charles Cotesworth, Missus Harriott brother, was a little boy, he play the violoncello in them St. Cecilia concert. Year after year that concert be the cock of the walk 'mongst society events in Chas'n—'cept durin' the war years. When General Francis Marion be a-runnin' up and down in the swamp, the society not have the concerts. But in 1787 the St. Cecilia rise right back up to the top of Chas'n society.

Missus Eliza and Missus Harriott take them young women down to Chas'n to King Street where the fancy dressmakers have their shops. All them Hampton women have beautiful gowns made to wear to them concert.

I tell you the truth, them dresses be somethin' to lay your eyas on. They be craft of the best cloth, what be wove of wool, hair, silk, hemp, flax, cotton, spun glass, and wire. I even hear tell of one gown what been made with threads of gold. The Hampton women dresses usually georgette, what be silk. The gowns have high neck, leg o' mutton sleeve, and bustles—and sometime a slight train what drag from the tail of the gown.

Them Hampton women twiss and twiss as they git into the gowns. They arch their back and squirm and wiggle it on. Then they sit at the glass as the servant work on their hair.

Women could not be members of that St. Cecilia Society. No. That distinction belong to the men. But women could attend the balls and concerts if they was kin to a member. Then even if their menfolk die, them women could still attend the concert.

That society 'lect its members at the annual meetin' by a letter presented by a member. Iffen a man father or gran'father or any of his close kin belong before him, there wasn't no doubt he would git in. But the members have to be of the *quality*. Iffen a new resident inquire 'bout membership, he be check out for good quality ancestors and such as that. When a man was chose, the names of the ladies of his household be put upon the list and remain there forever. Only thing erase them women name is their own death.

You see, Missus, that society be very straitlace. It was this way: time and season of the St. Cecilia was fix as if ordered by the heavenly bodies. Only Lent disturb its dates. Never have a ball on Saturday. No sirree. St. Cecilia ball always be held on Thursday. And always at nine o'clock in the evenin'.

The managers control ever'thing. No woman ever suggest or assist. Them same managers keep that up from year to year and leave their post only when they die.

The St. Cecilia Society have a old unwritten rule that ev'ry manager hold hisself 'countable for the pleasure and well-bein' of the guests. Ev'ry manager have a special charge, such as the floor, the music, the supper, and so on. It be on a man conscience if somethin' go wrong in his department. That be one secret of the society success.

Three balls was give in a season—one in January and two in February—carefully arrange to avoid touchin' upon Lent. Young ladies always 'rive at the ball with a chaperone, and the greatest decorum prevail. The latest bride be escort to the supper table by the president, and she feel she have achieve distinction.

And so all the missus of Hampton Plantation be on that old list, and they keep up that society habit and go down to Chas'n and git fancy gowns made to order. Ever'body see them at the concerts and know they been bearin' up, even in hard time.

The President Come A-Calling

Time come when Missus Eliza and Missus Harriott take a good look at Hampton house. As they stand in the yard and look toward the inland side of the mansion, they decide they need a new portico on that side of the house. Most visitors 'rive by boat, and the porch on the river side serve as the chief entry. The inland side been use as a racetrack, and now that side of the mansion was bein' neglect.

Missus Eliza say she remember the famous English actor David Garrick, from the time they was in England, and how he commission the Adam brothers to design a portico for his villa. She become so red hot with desire for that portico she could hardly talk about it. The two women light out 'cross the yard and look back at the mansion from afar. Missus Harriott say how beautiful a portico like that would be on Hampton house, and how dishearten she was in not havin' a avenue of oaks what would lead up to it.

Then and there she settle on gittin' rid of that racetrack and buildin' a portico. But they couldn't do nothin' 'bout that avenue of oaks. They look at the random oak trees, here and there, 'round and about, and say none was symmetrical. Then Missus Eliza call her daughter attention to one small oak a-growin' almost where the steps would be on the new portico. And she tell Missus Harriott that if President George Washington ever would come to Hampton, she was near'bout sure she would ask him what to do 'bout that oak. And then they branch out and talk 'bout President Washington and what it would be like iffen he would by chance come to Hampton.

Not long after that portico was underway, Missus Harriott and her mother decide to build a wing on each side of the mansion. On one side would be a two-story-high bedroom, and on the other side a ballroom what would be the envy of all the planters on the Santee River and in Chas'n.

When the portico was done, work begin on the wings. That ballroom come to be over two story high and have one-piece pine floorboards, each 'bout forty feet long. The fireplace in that room was line with colorful Delft tiles, showin' scenes to suit ev'ry taste. David and Golias and the Good Samaritan show up on them tiles.

One day, word come that President Washington be a-plannin' a visit to the coast of South Carolina. Missus Harriott and her mother go into a frenzy, makin' plans. Then a courier come and say that inns not be plentiful in the Low Country, and when the President visit he plan to take breakfast at Hampton. That be near'bout the best news they ever have. And they plan what to have for that breakfast. Missus Eliza remind Missus Harriott to ask the President to advise what to do 'bout that oak tree at the foot of the steps of the brand new portico.

That night in the drawing room, Missus Eliza bring out some cambric and say she gone make some bandeaux and sashes. When she git through with that, she embroider on them GOD BLESS OUR PRESIDENT and HAIL TO THE FATHER OF OUR COUNTRY.

It was in the year 1791 President George Washington show up in South Carolina and start his tour down the coast. Marse Thomas Pinckney, Missus Harriott brother, travel with him and the other bluebloods. The President have special feelin's for Marse Tomm and Marse Charles Cotesworth for many reason, but I hear tell the deep affection stem from the time in 1787 when Charles Cotesworth have a hand in helpin' draft the Constitution of the United States. And both brothers play a important part in gittin' the Federal Constitution ratify by the South Carolina Convention of 1788, what Marse Tomm preside over.

The day the President be expect for breakfast at Hampton, his party leave Georgetown early in the morning. It was a job gittin' 'cross the Sampit, North Santee, and South Santee River, because the President travel in a chariot with four horses and outriders. His favorite horse was led behind so he could change the exercise now and again. His luggage ride to the rear in a wagon. All the servant handsomely liveried.

As the President advance on his journey, all the gentry 'long the coast try to speak to him. And they follow that chariot to the next stoppin' place.

At Hampton Plantation on the day President Washington is to arrive, Missus Harriott and her daughter both be a-sittin' on high stools, dressin' their hair at the glass and weavin' their curls with the embroider headbands. Down the hall, Missus Eliza done ready, with headband and sash in place. She be fussin' with her gran'daughters, runnin' back and forth to the washstand, and askin', "Have you wash your face?"

One of the gran'daughters took it upon herself to look out for the procession, and she fly back and forth to the window seat to gaze 'cross the lawn. From that window she could see the carriage road and the gate. Carriages often brung guests to Hampton but none ever come bringin' visitors as important as President George Washington. After awhile, the niece see a carriage roll through the gate. She sound the alarm, and the women fly down the stairs and take their place on the portico steps.

Men on horseback and several carriages slowly pass by the porch. When the chariot bearin' the President arrive, it stop right in front. The Hampton women stand tall and straight as the President and Marse Tomm ascend three steps. The President was tall and spare and walk with the rollin' gait of a man who spend a lot of his time ridin' horses. Marse Tomm introduce the President to his mother and step aside.

Then President Washington say to Missus Eliza, "Madam, this is a meetin' to which I have long look forward. As a planter, I pay my respect to you for your early work with indigo and later with silk culture. You are both planter and patriot. Your sons truly reflect your love of principle, and their country will soon call them to even greater service. Mothers like you light fires that are never extinguish. As long as that happen, we have nothin' to fear for our Republic."

He bow low and hold Missus Eliza hand to his lips. Then he do the same with Missus Harriott and little Missus Harriott. Missus Harriott make a gesture for her nieces to approach, and she introduce them to the gentleman. He ask them if they was good girls, and Missus Eliza answer that indeed they was. One of the girls spat out that she knew four psalms by heart and would recite one of them. He chuckle, shake his head, and turn back to Missus Harriott. His face was square before her, and she later write to a friend that he had a face to remember. What a great nose! What a mouth! And what clear teeth! His face right away inspire confidence 'though his eyas was merry. The President turn to Missus Eliza, tuck her hand under his arm, and them two lead the way into the mansion.

In the ballroom the group feast on ham, egg, sausage, biscuit, shrimp, oyster from the marsh, and much more. For a short time all was quiet. The breakfast was a big success, much to Missus Harriott relief and she lean back in her chair and smile. Tinklin' laughter from the group drift out to the hall where the servants hear, and they talk 'bout that breakfast with the President and 'bout them quality women, Missus Eliza and Missus Harriott.

Then Missus Eliza survey the room so she can write 'bout her thoughts at a later time, when Missus Harriott also be recordin' ever'thing in her diary. Missus Eliza paint the very picture of that ballroom in her mind. The room was large and excessive tall, but there was nothin' too imposin' about it. It had its own beauty. Mirrors from France hung on the soarin' walls. Candles flickerin' from the table and window sills mellow the room. And even the high-flung white ceilin' blush in the rosy light reflectin' off the walls.

When President Washington say he believe it is time for the meal to end, he rise outen his seat and offer a toast to Missus Eliza and Missus Harriott. He mention their husbands and Missus Eliza sons. Then they all quit the ballroom.

As the President was standin' on the portico about to take his leave, Missus Harriott ask him 'bout that oak tree growin' at the steps. He say, "Leave it there and let it grow. Who can make a tree? Can you make one?" That tree been call "The Washington Oak" since that day, and it be there right now—today even.

Missus Eliza and Missus Harriott carry out their duty with worldly wisdom. Missus Eliza, Missus Harriott, and young Missus Harriott always talk 'bout President George Washington visit, and how the President look down the long cloth of white linen and watch Missus Harriott. Her manner and breedin' seem to astound him. But she attend to all her guest the same as to President Washington.

Now after all that excitement, Missus Eliza start talkin' 'bout being advance in years. She grieve over the death of her best friend, Lady Mary Mackenzie, who first marry Marse Drayton and next Marse Ainslie and lastly become the wife of Marse Henry Middleton. Lady Mary, what been the godmother of Missus Harriott, done gone to Glory at sea on her return from a visit to England.

Missus Eliza commence to think 'bout all the gone-on ones, all them who had ripen by her side. And she write to Marse Keate, her friend in England, and she talk 'bout all of that. She say that outlivin' them she love give the principal gloom to a long life. There was nothin' so appealin' to her in the prospect of old age, she say— the loss of friends bein' a loss she sorely felt. Missus Eliza go on to say in that letter that she could now see her children grown up, and, blessed be God, see them such as she had hope. "What is there in youthful enjoyment preferable to that?" she ask.

One mornin' Missus Eliza was feelin' poorly—not able to git out of bed. Missus Harriott say "Tilly-vally" and ever'body know that mean she was very upset. Missus Eliza play such a active role in the life of Hampton Plantation, Missus Harriott have trouble bearin' up when her mother come down sick. How heavy it woulda been on Missus Harriott shoulder iffen her mother had not help out durin' the war when Marse Daniel was away.

Missus Harriott run 'round and call the servants to come and look at Missus Eliza. But they not like sickness or to lay eyas on the dead decease, and they hang back in the hallway. The room and the house fall silent. And then Missus Eliza rally, and she say she so ill she believe she would like to go to Philadelphia, where she know some doctors what be skill in the profession of the physic.

Missus Harriott tell her servants to git ever'thing ready, and she take time to write in her diary how sick her mother is. She write a letter to Marse Tomm and Marse Charles Cotesworth. She also write to the Izard family in Philadelphia and to President George Washington. She send them letters out by a trusted servant to a planter friend she know would take care of the task of gittin' the letters on their way. She know in her heart the communication would be receive, and she would have help when she stand most in need. Then Missus Harriott git her mother into the coach where she rest on soft pillows. After they set out for the vessel, Missus Eliza gran'daughters stroke her, and Missus Harriott let them comfort their gran'mother and not interrupt.

The boat set sail for Phildelphia and after two day it come

upon a tempest-toss sea. The fear what grab them passenger when they know they be in the midst of a gale we can only imagine. That boat continuous roll this way and that, and them women pitch from side to side. Missus Harriott and her daughter and nieces be so careful of Missus Eliza and they stay with her day and night and hold her tight, but she have some mighty tumbles despite all her good care. The caretakers git toss about too and they go away from Missus Eliza when they check their own bruises and injuries, 'cause they not want her to see.

There was some talk by the boat crew 'bout the vessel founderin', and the women 'vision a swift close to their life. But the Good Lord put forth His hand and quiet that wind. The sea git calm and them women give thanks for their unexpect deliverance. Missus Harriott find her diary to write 'bout their adventure, but before she commence a-writin' she go back and read her last entry, what be, "Heaven help us."

When the vessel reach Philadelphia, Missus Eliza strain to open one eya to see Missus Izard coach at the landin'. Someone announce, "Congress is sittin'," and she try to raise up on one elbow, for she have interest in what Congress is doin'. But she fall back on her cot. Missus Izard coach take the women to the corner of Spruce and Third Street.

After Missus Eliza settle in, she begin to have visitors, but they was warn not to stay too long. Even President George Washington was told that. A doctor was a-sittin' in the hall outside the door, and servants go in and out, carryin' large bowls of artesian water. They dip cloth in that water and wring it out and put it on Missus Eliza forehead, what was burnin' up with fever. Some of the women who call on Missus Eliza was name Chew, Bingham, Harrison, and Cadwallader. The President of the United States call often, as did Secretary of the Treasury Alexander Hamilton. All of this please Missus Eliza, who continue to be a very sick woman. She whisper to Missus Harriott, "I am dyin'. They are a-comin' not for me but for my sons."

Missus Harriott stay with her mother most all the time. Missus Eliza lay weak and pale 'gainst a mound of pillows. Finally, the feverish glaze on her face fade, and she look more serene. Missus Harriott wash her face, fluff up the pillows, and brush her red-gold hair what now have silver threads 'mongst it. Before a visitor come in, Missus Harriott always carefully spread over her mother shoulder a green shawl, what 'tensify the mossiness of Missus Eliza eyas.

On the twenty-sixth day of May Missus Eliza take a turn for the worse, and after several hour in great agony, it please the Almighty to come a-callin'. Gentle, lovin' hands was all 'round her. And even though Marse Tomm was Minister to England and 'cross the sea and Marse Charles Cotesworth was back in South Carolina, Missus Eliza go to her rest support by them who love her.

President George Washington hurry to the deathbed, and he ask if he can be a pallbearer. Missus Harriott tell him that be a honor to her mother. The funeral was held in St. Peter churchyard in Philadelphia on the seventeenth day of May in 1793. President Washington, who was hisself sixty-one year old, help carry Missus Eliza to her grave.

Undaunted Daughter

After some time pass by, Missus Harriott take a close look at her daughter. 'Though Missus Eliza had radiate beauty with her red-gold hair and Missus Harriott been pretty enough, though not a great beauty, the young Missus Harriott was anything but a pretty woman. Her mother was grieve by her appearance, of course. Missus Harriott believe there was no power in her daughter nose and small, cherry mouth, and she saw no command in the eyas. Because of that, Missus Harriott think maybe her daughter would not fare good when it come to findin' a planter for a husband. And if she didn't find a planter to marry, she would never run a plantation manor house—just what she been groom for since she lay in the cradle. She would never direct a large number of servant or be host at large gatherin's or run a Chas'n house. She would never raise a child to teach her special brand of manners and principle to or to take her place in the world.

Young Missus Harriott been born in 1770, and was now past the time when plantation women gen'rally choose a husband and marry. Most plantation girls marry and start a fam'ly before their twentieth year.

If you remember, Missus, in that book *Gone with the Wind*, Missus Ellen O'Hara, Missus Scarlett mother, was consider middle-age by the time she was thirty year. That I can't forgot, 'cause Marse Clark Gable come to Hampton Plantation before that picture show was made, and I remember all 'bout that.

Missus Harriott think hard. When most plantation women was of the age of her daughter, they be runnin' huge estates and have several head of children. Of all the tribulation Missus Harriott suffer, no pain ever hit her as hard as her daughter station in life. The girl didn't seem to have no station. Missus Harriott never be one to do any devilment, but she was determine to do somethin' 'bout her daughter future.

Missus Harriott have other worries too. I always say, "Don't worry worry 'til worry worries you," but Missus Harriott fret over Hampton. 'Though she could live at the plantation for the rest of her days, there was nothin' to guarantee her son and his wife wouldn't return from France and claim Hampton as their home. That would bring in another missus, and two missus not fare well. While worryin' 'bout her daughter, she make a decision 'bout her own life.

Marse Thomas Ferguson, a large landowner in the Parish of St. Paul, put his Chas'n mansion on the market. That house was on Tradd Street and in the midst of mansions own by people of the quality. Beside being in such a uppity neighborhood, the house bear the mark of a British cannonball what been fire into the town in 1780. When Missus Harriott go to Chas'n, she take a look at the Ferguson mansion and buy it for herself. From then on, that house be the Chas'n mansion where she hold forth.

One day young Missus Harriott was sittin' at her dressin' table in the Chas'n mansion when her mother come in. "Gittin' your hair ready for the ball?" she ask.

"Yas," the daughter say.

"May I help you?" the mother ask.

The young girl just been knockin' 'round with it anyway, and without answerin', she hand her mother the brush.

Missus Harriott study her daughter face and then she brush out the long hair. She decide to try somethin' new, and she start the tortu'ous task of shakin' all that hair into a grand *coiffure*.

As she work on the hair, she look again at her daughter face. It was unnatural pale, spare of any powder or French rouge what most young women then favor. The young missus 'bout look sick—ashen skin and lips. The mother was stupefied.

Suddenly Missus Harriott realize she was gapin' at her daughter, and that was the height of rude. But she couldn't help herself. That face start to haunt her.

Missus Harriott was deep in her thinkin' as she roll the heavy hair 'round into the pompadour, but she casually say, "Your hair is so lovely you will surely attract the 'tention of some young planter at the ball tonight."

The daughter just spit out that she didn't want a planter. She say there be too many planters in the Horry family already, both men *and* women.

Her mother stop workin' on the hair, and her face have a forlorn look. She detect raw nerves bein' barely control, but she decide to give her daughter somethin' to study on. She tell her all daughters of planters marry young planters, and they marry early, 'fore they twenty. It was the architecture of the system, she say, and her daughter must follow that old plan.

The daughter scream out that the old architecture may have been the scheme of things up to that time, but she was not a schemin' person. She was different. She go on to say that she may or may not attract a *young planter*, as her mother say, but if she not marry a planter it would not be the death of her.

Missus Harriott finish the hair, and it was the elegant pompadour what was the height of fashion in London. Missus Harriott always take notice of the hairstyles in the newspapers from that place. She always read 'bout the cookin' receipts, styles, and stories in them English papers.

Missus Harriott give her daughter hair a pat, then she stand back and ask young Missus Harriott just what she mean by her words.

The daughter say again that if she didn't marry a planter it would not be the death of her.

Missus Harriott walk over to the bed, sit down, and gaze back at her daughter face in the looking glass above the dressin' table. She say that sometime she believe her daughter was like one of her ancestors.

The daughter ask who she talkin' about.

Missus Harriott go on and say that one of her daughter ancestor been a pirate and all he thought 'bout was goin' to sea. She say he had not a speck of sense for plannin' for a plentiful life.

The daughter jump up and scream out, "A pirate?"

"Yas," her mother answer.

The daughter say she never heard one word 'bout such a thing. There was never mention of one of her ancestors bein' a pirate.

Missus Harriott start that old story talkin' 'bout her brother, Marse Thomas Pinckney. She say that Marse Tomm been name for Thomas Pinckney, of Bishop Auckland, county Durham, England. He come to South Carolina in the *Loyal Jamaica* in April of 1692. He had live in the West Indies and the story was told that he engage in privateerin'. His affidavit, date the twenty-second day of August

1692, say that Thomas Pinckney, gentleman, age twenty-four year, belong to the sloop *Dyamond* at the time that sloop and the *Mary* capture a French vessel what was condemn at Port Royal, Jamaica, and sold.

Missus Harriott stop talkin' and look at her daughter, who was takin' all of it in. "I could show you the records," the mother say, "but they was destroy durin' the British attack on Tomm's house on the Ashepoo River."

The daughter say she could not believe her uncle been name for a pirate.

Missus Harriott say her brother bring distinction to the fam'ly. Never once did she believe it would be otherwise. And, yas, he was name after the pirate Thomas Pinckney.

Then Missus Harriott go on to say that her daughter was not the only woman in the fam'ly who was takin' her time in catchin' a husband. Two of her nieces was late in makin' a choice. She say she was concern 'bout Maria Henrietta and Harriott Pinckney. They just hang back. But at least her other niece, Eliza Lucas, was castin' her eya at blueblood. Missus Harriott say she been thinkin' 'bout that off and on, and she want them young women to remember that planters from the best fam'lies marry early.

Then Missus Harriott drop a thunderbolt of surprise. She tell her daughter she had bought a track of land on the South Santee River, not far from Hampton. Downriver from Fairfield and Peachtree Plantations. She say she was gone build a mansion there, one quite comfortable for a fam'ly—'cept it wouldn't be for *her* fam'ly.

"And pray tell, whose is it?" her daughter ask.

Missus Harriott say the new plantation would belong to her daughter. She may not marry a planter and acquire a plantation by the usual way, Missus Harriott go on, but she *would* be the mistress of a fine plantation of her very own.

Oh, how the daughter squeal 'bout that. She say, "Mother, you wouldn't!"

And Missus Harriott yell, "I already have."

The daughter ask who the field workers would be, and Missus Harriott answer that she had give that some thought. There was plenty of people in her labor force, and she would divide them between Hampton and the new place.

The daughter protest that they be give double task.

Missus Harriott really come down on her daughter for that. She say the people at Hampton always have a easy time of it, 'specially when compare with other plantations. No one would have a double task.

The daughter shoot back with harsh words. She say she would hand it to her mother that Hampton servants wasn't made to eat ash cake and drink persimmon beer, but she not want them to have to clear out that river jungle for any rice field, much less her very own rice field.

"That has already been done," Missus Harriott announce.

Then the daughter say she like that pirate. He was independent, and he didn't care if the people in South Carolina not approve of his work. She say she prob'ly did inherit his likeness and she was glad of that.

Missus Harriott answer, "Tilly-vally!" She say that word, you know, only when she was upset.

The daughter cry and say again she was like the pirate and she was glad.

Missus Harriott heart musta gone out to her daughter and feel she had deal her a hard blow, tellin' her 'bout the new plantation and all of that. And knowin' she would not see that pirate on this side of the world, she talk 'bout him some more. She say that soon after the pirate Thomas Pinckney 'rive in South Carolina, he marry Grace Bedon, a daughter of some famous man name of George Bedon. It was a good marriage, and the bond was date the nineteenth day of September, 1692. But that wife die, and the pirate marry another: Mary Cotesworth, the daughter of Charles Cotesworth of Durham, England.

Young Missus Hariott want to know if the pirate finally become a planter. She ask if he was said to be of the quality.

He did not become a planter, her mother explain, but a merchant in Chas'n. However, he was regard as one of the landed gentry as he was born to the quality and he own considerable land on the Ashepoo and Ashley Rivers. He own some city lots too.

Did he have any children? the daughter want to know.

"Yas," her mother say, "children by both his wives. A son of his second wife, Mary Cotesworth, was your gran'father Charles Pinckney."

"You mean my gran'father" the daughter cry out, "was the son of a pirate?"

"Yas," Missus Harriott answer, with no apology.

And the daughter say she had love her gran'mother Eliza Lucas Pinckney more than anyone, and she would have love her gran'father too. She say she was like her gran'father and his father, the pirate.

Afterwhile, the two women finally cool off.

Young Missus Harriott was walkin' in the yard at Hampton Plantation one day when she come upon a girl from the quarters name Sarah holdin' a bottle of whiskey in her hand. Little Missus Harriott ask what she was doin' with that whiskey, and the girl say old Tom give it to her.

"I sure want to drink it, Missus Harriott, but I 'fraid to."

"Why are you 'fraid to drink it?" Young Missus Harriott ask her.

"Tom is old and cripple, and I'se a young woman. He want me to love him. I 'fraid he put conjure in the drink to make me love him."

"Why do you not just pour the whiskey on the ground?" Missus Harriott come back.

"'Cause I want to drink it. I not often git good whiskey," Sarah say.

"You like me to strain it for you?" Missus Harriott offer.

"Yas'm. You do that," Sarah reply.

Little Missus Harriott take the bottle of whiskey and strain it. Sure 'nough, there was bits of cut up hair, string, chips, and other thing what go to make up the conjure. Sarah take the whiskey and drink it in one gulp, but she never give old Tom a glance after that conjure business.

Little Missus Harriott git all interest in conjurin', and one day she ask Sarah to tell her 'bout the superstitions 'mongst the people of the quarters. Sarah trust the young missus because she strain that whiskey, so she tell her what she know.

Mustard sprinkle 'round the house scare away ghosts. If you carry a bottle of whiskey at night, be sure to pour a little on the ground for the ghost to lap up; otherwise, the ghost empty your bottle before you git home, cork or no cork. If a owl hoot near your house, put a straw in your hair—the straw prevent bad luck comin' to you. Never burn Spanish moss; that for sure bring bad luck. Plantin' cedar trees near your house is bad luck. Iffen you do, one in your fam'ly gone die for each cedar tree been plant.

There was many superstition what Sarah tell little Missus Harriott, but the one she think on most was if a horse or mule pass your house and turn it head and hee-haw, someone in the house soon marry. Little Missus Harriott never did see a horse do that at Hampton house. She been give up on a-marryin', planter or no planter.

But her mother never give up on her own plans. Missus Harriott be busy with the plantin' of rice and the buildin' of the house at the new plantation. Her daughter not carry on somethin' scandalous 'bout it, but she pay it no attention.

Plantation for an Old Maid

A-sendin' and receivin' mail in them day and time be a task, Missus, and that's for sure. Each year the Christmas season bring with it a increase burden of mail what must be deliver prompt to people scatter 'bout the Union. There was no place too remote for mail to reach—iffen the slightest clue to the where'bouts of the person for whom it was intend had been supply by the sender. That connects with the old story Mark Twain used to tell. Upon receivin' a letter address to him at "God knows where" he chuckle and say, "He did!" God *did* know where he was to receive that mail.

Letters was not brought to Chas'n by stagecoach 'til 'bout 1860, so many of Missus Harriott friend not know she been pourin' over plans with builders on a house for her daughter, the old maid.

In gittin' wood for the new house, them builders take the old broad axe and cut down big trees in the swamp. Missus Harriott give her close attention to ev'ry detail durin' the buildin', but her daughter pay no nevermind. Missus Harriott believe with all her heart when the house be complete, her daughter will love and cherish it and become a fine mistress.

The 'leventh day of October come and it was a nice fall day. As the day wane, Missus Harriott think 'bout the party she would plan for her daughter. As she was sittin' and thinkin' she notice a courier a-comin' into the Hampton yard. She go weak in the knees, for it wasn't ev'ry day a courier bring a message to Hampton. The first courier what come to the plantation, you remember, Missus, tell her that George Washington would eat breakfast there. So Missus Harriott run to the porch to find out what this courier have on his mind. She see the message in his hand, but bein' a lady of manners and principle she ask would he like to rest up a bit. She tell him someone would come and take his horse to the water trough. He hand her the paper.

Missus Harriott go into the drawin' room, sit down, and open the letter. She read it through quicklike, and then she read it again. It was a lovin' letter, at that. It start out, "Dearest Mother." And then it go on to say that the daughter had elope with Frederick Rutledge. She spoke of his fam'ly. He was a son of John Rutledge and a nephew of Edward Rutledge who sign the Declaration declarin' the colonies to be free and independent of England. Then she say, "Oh, Mother, you know how much I love Harrietta. It is so lovely. It has your touch. You must find some use for it. Frederick and I shall live in his home in Chas'n." And she sign it, "Yours, with all the love in my heart, Harriott."

Now, Missus, Harrietta Plantation be a-settin' over there on the South Santee River empty and unfinish. No one a-livin' in it. But when the next spring come, Missus Harriott send her hands over there to work the rice fields. So when fall arrive there was a good income from that plantation. Missus Harriott have a nice new plantation, whether her daughter live there or not, and she never seem to care one way or the other 'bout that. Harrietta Plantation stand empty, but Missus Harriott not blink a eye because she so happy 'bout her daughter choice of husband. Of all the South Carolina blueblood, she had chose a husband from the very top. But Missus Harriott worry and fret whether her daughter adapt to becomin' a plantation mistress.

The First Begin of the Rutledge

Missus Harriott take care of all the plantation business, and then she go to her Chas'n mansion, where she be near her daughter. Them two ride all over Chas'n in that fine carriage and spend their time a-doin' good. Missus Harriott means, of course, was ample and to give money was a easy thing. But that was not the biggest charity what live in her tender heart. With her own hands she fix large mug of tea and coffee with bread on top of each, and them two women take that to the needy neighborhoods of Chas'n. 'Most ev'ry day that carriage, what was pull by four beautiful matchin' bay horses, go out and it be seen not at some uppity store on King Street but at homes of the poor and sufferin'. Not ever'body in the fam'ly know 'bout that charity work, but me old Missus tell me all 'bout that. It be a well-kept secret.

Missus Harriott and her daughter and son-in-law enjoy goin' to the theater. They go to 'most ev'ry play what appear in Chas'n. The old theater was situate on Broad Street, not too far from Missus Harriott mansion on Tradd Street. All the quality people go to the theater in that day and time. After a play have a good run in England, it usually come to Chas'n to entertain the aristocracy.

Marse Thomas Sully, a artist from England, was beginnin' his work in Chas'n. After finishin' a hard day work a-paintin' the likeness of a member of a planter fam'ly, he attend the theater. Marse Sully play in one of the pantomimes, and he jump through a clock. The Chas'n people can scarse believe he do that, and he begin to be thought of as a big sport—somethin' they never consider him to be 'fore that jump.

When someone was ask to play a part in a play, if that person was a tolerable good mimic, he would accept. Usually the theatergoers saw some of their friend on the stage. The theater never take the place of the horse races and the St. Cecilia events but it was popular. The manager of the old theater was a man name Marse Gilfert, and he was always ask to play the role of a gentleman who look over his spectacles at the audience. Each time he do that, the audience was right joyous.

Marse Gilfert also figure in another bit of drama. He live in a very good suite of apartment in the theater. Marse Jarvis, a celebrate portrait painter, was his friend. One day, while a-visitin' with Marse Gilfert, Marse Jarvis say he bet he could paint Marse Gilfert likeness by the time he walk to the place where mail be receive and sort and return to the theater.

Marse Gilfert take the bet on condition that the likeness be instantly recognize by mutual friends. Marse Gilfert send for Marse Fred to be witness and Marse Fred bring his wife and mother-in-law to the theater.

Marse Jarvis made ready, mixin' his colors and puttin' the canvas before him. He take the brush in his hand and tell Marse Gilfert to be off.

Marse Gilfert start with the speed of a quarter horse. He go down Broad Street with a stride he was not wont to have, 'complishin' the distance in a short time for a ordinary man. But Marse Jarvis had not been slow in his paintin'.

When Marse Gilfert return, the witness ask to see the likeness. Marse Jarvis have his friend on the canvas within the time specify. No one could mistake the bold outline he had dash off.

Marse Gilbert pay the bet cheerfully, sayin' he always thought he was *a man of mark* and now he was satisfy he was so. Otherwise, his likeness couldn'ta been so quick to take.

Marse Fred and the two Missus Harriott often saw Marse Gilfert in plays. He was their very favorite. They call him "a star."

After all of that, it come to pass that Missus Harriott daughter and Marse Fred decide to go to Hampton and live with Missus Harriott. They never give one thought to livin' at Harrietta. No. They go to Hampton Plantation, and there prob'ly be several reasons for that. Maybe they feel that Missus Harriott need a man to help her run both them plantations, as her brothers not be in position to help.

You want to know what Marse Tomm been up to? Marse Tomm go to London, and while there his name was place on the ticket as a candidate for the vice president with John Adams. When he return home he learn that Adams had win the president and Thomas Jefferson the vice president. Marse Tomm then been elect to Congress. After that he marry Missus Frances Motte Middleton, a sister of his first wife. They be a couple to take notice of. Not only was

Marse Tomm the master of Fairfield and El Dorado Plantations, he help his new wife build a London-style mansion on George Street in Chas'n, a lot what been convey to her father in 1770. To the original lot she add a lot on the west, and she begin to build the London-style house. After she marry Marse Tomm, together they complete the house, and the total cost was $53,800.

Missus Harriott other brother, Marse Charles Cotesworth, been in France where he serve a important post for what President George Washington send him. Both Missus Harriott brother have so much responsibility she hesitate to call on them, but she keep up with them, sure 'nough.

Missus Harriott daughter and Marse Fred think on all of that and they realize Missus Harriott need help with runnin' two large plantation. But I 'specs there was another reason for them to move back to Hampton. They was 'spectin' their first child.

Missus Harriott was right there when that child drop from the daughter. He be christen Edward Cotesworth Rutledge. Two year later, in 1800, Frederick Rutledge been born, and the very next year the first daughter, who be name Elizabeth Pinckney. Then the young Missus Harriott drop Harriott Pinckney, Maria, and Thomas Pinckney. In 1809 she drop John Henry, and the last child was Eliza Lucas. By 1810 Marse Fred and Missus Harriott have eight head of children. Hampton Plantation never be more alive than then and in the years what follow.

Now you think 'bout that, Missus. That daughter what be believe would never even marry, now be marry to a prominent man and she be the mother of eight head of children. That be somethin' to dwell on, I tell you this mornin'.

And there was somethin' else 'bout that daughter was mighty important. Sometime durin' them years of childbearin', somethin' happen to young Missus Harriott that make her mother the happiest person on this earth. The daughter come 'round to think on things the same as the mother.

They say the old system of first-born inheritin' die out but, Missus, that not be true in most fam'ly I hear tell of. Missus Harriott and her daughter both believe it important for all girl baby to be brought up right and marry a planter. All boy baby be train to look after a plantation and become a wealthy planter, even them who do not inherit the fam'ly property. And the boy baby be 'spec to grow up and marry such women as them who father own large planta- tion. Then they have two fam'ly seat, and from all of that they be sure to find a plantation for their own.

Missus Harriott and her daughter raise them Rutledge chil- dren right. They be taught manners and principle without ceasin', and they be coach on who to marry. That be one of the most impor- tant lesson they learn. You remember, Missus, that the daughter once say she want to be like a pirate and she not believe in all them plantation teachin's? Well, she forgot about that old fuss she have with her mother and they come to be of one mind 'bout all them thing, and she and her mother become close. And both them women teach the lesson to the little Rutledge children.

The young Rutledge boys go fishin' and huntin' 'most ev'ry day 'cept Sunday. There was creeks and inlets and the big Santee River to furnish many a happy hour a-fishin'. The inlets furnish saltwater fish, and they was the scene of merry fishin' parties. Fish fries in the summer and oyster roasts in the winter was enjoy by large and small group.

For the fish fry, cornbread, pickle, and sauce was carry from home. Coffee was cook on the ground. Iffen the party was large, some of them go on ahead to secure the fish. For the meal, the fish was roll in cornmeal and lower into a huge iron kettle of sizzlin' hot fat. After a few minutes they was brought up, golden brown, ready to eat.

For the oyster roast, milk, butter, bread, salt and pepper, pickle, and coffee was carry from home. An oyster stew was sometime desire. The oyster was carry from the marsh beforehand. Two fire was build. One was for the stew and coffee and was build beneath a stove, what was actually a sheet of iron set up 'bout ten inch from the ground on four leg. The other fire was for roastin' the oyster and heatin' water to put them oyster in so they could be open for the stew. While the stew was a-cookin', them folk skill at openin' the oyster kept the company supplied with roast ones. Ever'one who try it have no dispute the best part of the meal was a pipin' hot oyster just open and presented on a pipin' hot half shell, with pickle and cornbread.

The day was top off with canoein' and explorin' along the river edge.

Durin' this time, Missus, Marse John Henry, the seventh child of Marse Fred and Missus Harriott, become attach to his mother and gran'mother. The gran'mother say he was so sweet that sugar just naturally roll offen him. When all them children go a-fishin', John Henry hang back. He look at his mother and gran'mother on the steps of Hampton house a-wavin' good-bye. He go back and kiss them ev'ry time. Some of the time he would kiss them and run back to his brothers and sisters, then he would hesitate and go back to the steps for a second kiss. Oh, how them women did love that child. That was somethin' in this world, the way they love that child.

A Heart as Light as the Breast Feather of a Turkey

The coastal land on which Marse John Henry live offer all kind of adventure.

One day he have a powerful urge to take a canoe and go to a offshore island where he could explore the beach. His first incline was to take his small canoe, made in one-piece from a single cypress tree, and go alone. Instead, he invite Esau, a son of slaves, to go with him.

'Bout midafternoon, the two set out. One boy paddle from one side of the boat, and the other paddle from the other side. The canoe move forward through the water much faster than they had believe it would.

As they glide down the Santee River, the goin' was easy. But once they had leave the mainland and start for the island, the goin' git kinda rough. The ocean and the actual breakers was on the east side of the island, and Esau and Marse John Henry had to use all the stren'th they could muster to git that boat 'round to the ocean side. After they did that, they beach the vessel and hotfoot it across the sand.

The boys walk along 'til they come to that old wrack line, where there was a mess of driftwood, bleach seashells, whelk egg cases, pieces of sponge, and a pile of starfish. Marse John Henry ask Esau to help him gather up some specimens to take home, but Esau have in mind runnin' down the beach where he saw somethin' in the distance.

Marse John Henry say he beat him there, and they strike out in a run. When they reach the object what had wash in from the sea, they see a huge loggerhead turtle, but someone had whittle out the insides and left only the shell. Marse John Henry wanta take that shell home, but Esau try to talk him out of that, a-tellin' him it be 'bout as smelly as anything. But Marse John Henry mind made up and he pick up that old turtle shell and head toward the canoe.

All the time they was a-walkin' back to the boat, Esau was a-tellin' Marse John Henry that his mother was gonna rake him over the hot coals for a-bringin' home a smelly old thing such as that. But Marse John Henry say his mother never scold him in his entire life and neither had his gran'mother.

Esau ask him 'bout his gran'mother, for Missus Harriott been like the queen of the South Carolina Low Country, but Marse John Henry say she was just *gran'mother*.

"She sho treat people good," Esau say.

Marse John Henry say, yas, he know that and he hope all the people on the plantation was good to them who work in the rice field. Esau say he wouldn't give a crust for some of them, but he never say who that was.

Esau say he had two sisters, name of Eph and Kizzie, and they live close to the spring where his ma did their washin'. And then he spoke of his great-gran'mother, who he said would be one hundred sixteen year old and could eat as hard a bread as any of them.

Marse John Henry believe that Esau was enjoyin' talkin' 'bout the folk he sprung from more than a-visitin' the beach, so Marse John Henry ask him some more about them.

Esau tell Marse John Henry that his great-gran'mother Veenia been pirate-captured, and he tell that story with pride. Marse John Henry ask where they was a-livin' at the time, and Esau say they live at a plantation near Chas'n. He say the pirate gone to the Missus and take all the money. Then the pirate take Missus and Esau great-gran'mother on his boat. Gran'mother Ma—that what Esau call her—been scared. She twiss and twiss and turn herself in the Missus skirt. The pirate put them off 'round Georgetown and after that they live at Hampton Plantation.

Right that minute, Marse John Henry start to like Esau better than any other person outside his own fam'ly.

After they git that old turtle shell in the boat, they go back and collect some of them seashells. I don't know the name of all of them, Missus, but some was clam shell, and others be call snail. Some was plain, while others was fancy, and they was of all color. When the boat was 'bout full of shells, them boys go back toward the wrack line, and their eyas fall on a stand of what they call the old witch trees. They run on their bare feet into that stand.

Them trees be witchy all right and they cast long shadows on the sandy beach. Just then Marse John Henry find a old green bottle. He pull it out of the sand and tell Esau he plan to take it home. They didn't look at the bottle real good but Marse John Henry tuck it under his arm.

They start to talk 'bout the plants what been sturdy enough to stand against salt and high tides, and Marse John Henry point out the old pennywort vine and sea kale and panic grass. He put down the bottle and pick a bouquet of sea kale while he 'splain to Esau how the plants been doin' their job of bondin' the sand together.

Next they turn their attention to the birds a-wheelin' in the sky. They talk 'bout them lonesome wails and wonder what the birds be lonesome for. Esau ask where them bird lay their eggs and Marse John Henry say some of them nest be no more than slight impressions in the sand. Esau say he gone watch his step. Marse John Henry tell him that be a good idea, 'specially 'cause they would likely see a snake 'fore they git home. That subject bring Esau to suggest they return home.

As they make their way back to the canoe they talk 'bout how the dunes be kept up by all the green growth, what look like tiny forests of prickly pear and yucca and little rosettes of dune thistle.

Once the boys was in the canoe and headin' back toward the mainland, darkness fall in quick. They had not seen a snake, but they witness fence lizards and spiders and some wasp.

Marse John Henry say he didn't believe Esau wanta come back to that place, and Esau say he wanta go back and look again where they found the bottle. His great-gran'mother had told him all his life that pirates hid treasure on the offshore islands near Hampton Plantation. As the bottle was found there, it could be a place where a pirate treasure been bury.

At that moment, Marse John Henry remember he put down his bottle to pick the bouquet of sea kale and he start a-turnin' that canoe 'round. He say he was goin' back. Esau tell him it was too late to be a-goin' back and they had to git home. But, no, that did not suit Marse John Henry. He had to go back right that minute 'cause he believe the bottle would not be there the next day.

The sun been gone down by the time the boys beach the canoe, and they run as fast as they can to the witch trees. There was the bottle, zackly where Marse John Henry put it. He pick it up and they fly back to the canoe. By the time the boys was a-crossin' over to the mainland, it was so dark they could hardly see how to guide the boat. The goin' was not only rough, it was slow.

Esau was the first to stop talkin'. He just paddle and paddle and not say anything. Marse John Henry quit talkin' too, and he work just as hard. Finally, they find a place along the Santee River to beach the boat and they pull it up into the bush. Marse John Henry grab that bottle and bouquet, and he start a-flyin' home.

'Fore he git to the house, he see a lantern comin' through the woods. His brother Fred voice call out, "John Henry! John Henry!"

Marse John Henry answer that he was there. He ask Marse Fred if his mother and gran'mother was anxious. His brother say they was out of their mind. Marse John Henry start to cry and he run so fast he leave his brother and Esau behind. When he reach the house, his mother and gran'mother be a-standin' on the steps. They was frantic with worry. Marse John Henry hand his mother the bottle and bouquet and put his arms 'round her waist. He sob that he never mean to hurt her.

You know somethin', Missus? Them women could not scold Marse John Henry for bein' gone 'cause they believe his heart was broke. It was broke all right 'cause he had worry his mother and gran'mother. They try to calm him down, and they tell him the sun just go down faster than usual and none of it was his fault. But his face sag in worriment. Finally, he say he would never in his life do anything to upset them again. The two women work near half the night a-tryin' to soothe that boy.

When things quiet down, they all look at the bottle Marse John Henry pick up, and his mother see a tiny note inside it. She pull out the stopper and they work for a hour a-tryin' to git that note out. At last, they retrieve it.

The note, a-scribble by a man name of Dr. Tyre, say iffen anyone find that note to know it had been drop in the sea at Africa. Marse John Henry was so proud of it he almost forgot 'bout how he had worry his mother. She stroke his head and tell him she was gone start a plantation museum, and that note and bottle be the focal point.

Then Marse John Henry tell her 'bout the canoe full of seashells and the turtle shell, and how he would go to the boat tomorrow and tote them home. She say she would like to display all of that on a shelf out in the kitchen. That would always be known as the John Henry Rutledge Museum, she say. Finally, Marse John Henry git back to normal, and he tell his mother and gran'mother how much he love them. Then he go upstairs to bed in his room what be at the very top of the stairway.

Them women sit up, a-shakin' their heads. They talk about Marse John Henry and say what a sensitive child he is. None of the other children be anything at all like that. Them other children snicker and make fun of Marse John Henry, but he didn't care what they did so long as he please his mother and gran'mother.

Them women declare that from that time on they would have to be 'specially tender with that child. They say he was the sweetest child they ever know, and they would never in the world do anything to hurt him. They have to watch themselves and treat him as though his heart was the breast feather of a turkey. It was so light, it just float 'round, waitin' for somebody to crush it.

Plantation Hunter

Missus, Marse John Henry love the outdoor with all his heart. When night come, he read the books in the library—stories 'bout elephant, moose, tiger, rhino, and such as that. And when first light come, he be outside, enjoyin' the wildlife on the plantation. He content hisself with humble game.

His oldest brother, Marse Edward Cotesworth, been thinkin' 'bout joinin' the Navy. He always like ships. And Marse Edward be very fond of his uncle Charles Cotesworth Pinckney, Missus Harriott brother, and he spend time with him. The next brother, Marse Frederick, be a agriculturist like his great-gran'mother, Eliza Lucas Pinckney, Missus Harriott mother.

Missus Eliza, you remember, be the one who start up the production of indigo in South Carolina. Her father, who been governor of Antigua, send her some indigo plants. And she start up the plantin' of indigo what make many South Carolina planters rich. She also start up the production of silk, but that didn't last long in South Carolina. She save some of them bolts of silk cloth she make to the end of her life. Missus Eliza also start a fig orchard, what in her letters she spell *figg*. And now her gran'son Marse Fred like to plant just like she did.

The other brother, Thomas, and the girls, just been preoccupy with parties, races, and courtin', like other young blueblood.

But Marse John Henry, he just love the outdoor, and his mother and gran'mother never advise him to change 'bout that. But they advise him near'bout all the time who he must marry. Missus Harriott tell him that Hampton Plantation still be own by her son Daniel, who now go by the name Charles Lucas Pinckney Horry, over in France. 'Though he have no children, they not know when he might come home and claim that plantation.

His gran'mother go on to say that iffen her son in France die, he would likely leave the plantation to her. And after she die Marse John Henry oldest brother, Marse Edward Cotesworth, would own the property. 'Course Marse Edward not care anything at all for it, 'cause he love the Navy.

Marse John Henry gran'mother go on to say that iffen he would never own Hampton Plantation, the thing for him to do would be marry a planter daughter. And he could start a-sowin' them seeds anytime, as plenty young girl was comin' to Hampton for parties. If his luck fall right, he would find one to his likin', she say.

But Marse John Henry never cast a glance toward them girl. By the time he was six Marse John Henry was a-bringin' game home for the table. And when he was eight his mother depend on him to provide them with wild turkey, venison, quail, and other game. Marse John Henry believe with all his heart there was no better time to be had in all the land than huntin' at Hampton Plantation. 'Though he was the head man when it come to puttin' game on the table, he look at it as just havin' a good time.

'Long 'bout that time Marse John Henry mother commence writin' a journal 'bout his huntin' adventures. Each time he git home after a hunt, he sit down and tell her ever'thing, ev'ry little detail and she write it all down.

Me old Missus tell me all of that, and I always like to listen to them words. That be why I remember the detail. That I can't forgot.

Each fall of the year, ducks come down from the cold region of the No'th. When them clouds of duck descend on the rice field, the sky turn black in the middle of the day. Marse John Henry have only to point his gun toward the sky. ***Bang! Bang!*** and he bring down a boatload. The cooks at Hampton know how to roast a duck, let me tell you, and to make cornbread dressin'. They mash up peanuts and put that into the dressin'. Just the smell of a duck roastin' was enough to bring people to the kitchen at Hampton.

One mornin' after breakfast, as the frost was beginnin' to disappear, Marse John Henry go a-huntin' quail with Esau. When they come to the broom grass at the edge of a rice field, Marse John Henry say quail likely to roost there, so they wait. Sure 'nough, in no time at all, a covey take wing. The bird fly straight down the edge of the field, not goin' more than a hundred yard. Marse John Henry say they was 'bout to rise again, and he'd be ready for them.

"You know, iffen I don't git meat for the table, all my fam'ly is a-sittin' there with nothin' to eat," Marse John Henry tell Esau. "We live near 'bout twenty mile from the store, and I'm a-gone put meat on that table ev'ry day."

Esau listen to that spiel and not say anything. Just then that covey rise, and Marse John Henry shoot. He hit four. But four little bird was precious little for that Hampton table. He shoot again, and this time he miss clean. Then the birds turn toward the river, knowin' that safety be on the other side of that water. Marse John Henry raise his gun again and this time double his bag—which was not hard as there musta been forty bird. He got four more. "Well, I have somethin' for dinner, anyhow," he say.

On the way home, Esau say he like to take a rabbit to his fam'ly. They be a-walkin' along a field of broom grass when they spook a swamp rabbit, what is smaller than a regular rabbit and have no white meat on him. Marse John Henry take aim and make a hit. He tell Esau to go git him.

'Though their highest hopes was unfulfill, they head toward home.

Dinner was 'bout three o'clock in the afternoon. Marse John Henry take his place at the table, already a-thinkin' 'bout his next hunt. He always have a late afternoon hunt, as well as a early mornin' one. Them quail sure did dress up that dinner table, all cook to a golden brown and serve in a thin gravy, with hot biscuits.

Late in the day Esau and Marse John Henry set out again. They love that time of day in the pinelands, so they head that direction. Turnin' off the road a mile from home, they separate'long the edge of Montgomery Branch to wait and watch. Bein' a hundred or so yard apart, they had a little system of signals what allow them to communicate the presence of game.

As all sounds come in clear durin' that time of day, the two boys could hear gray squirrels barkin' from the trees above and people talkin' and children playin' far as two mile away. Just then a great flight of blackbird sweep 'cross the sky, headin' for the marsh. A sudden soft whistle bring Marse John Henry to attention and he start movin' toward Esau. When Marse John Henry git to him, Esau

have a big fox squirrel treed in a pine. Marse John Henry bring him
down with one shot and he give that squirrel to Esau.

Marse John Henry suggest they change position, and they did.
Just as they settle down, another flight of blackbird sweep past overhead. That time Marse John Henry bring down nine. At last he have
somethin' in his bag to take home. Nothin' disappoint him more
than goin' home and havin' his brother and sister ask what he bring
them, and he have to tell them he had not had a successful shot.

As Esau and Marse John Henry reach a cornfield, what also
have peas planted in it, they see flock after flock of dove headin'
for a certain sunny corner near a pine thicket. Marse John Henry
tell Esau to stay in the field and he go hide in the thicket to wait for
the dove to come in. Esau never object to anything Marse John
Henry tell him to do, as they was good friends.

Marse John Henry was ready when them bird start comin' toward him. After his first shot, there musta been two hundred birds
what scatter in all direction. But they not go far. They was hungry,
and Marse John Henry know they soon be back. Meanwhile, Esau
keep a-stirrin' them up from the other part of the cornfield, and
some come the way of Marse John Henry. After 'bout an hour in the
thicket, he bring down a dozen dove.

On the way home, Marse John Henry say he cannot bring home
deer and turkey ev'ry time he go out. Sometime his fam'ly have to
go on small game. Beside, he say, he have plenty game for the table.
"I'd a-rather see blackbird and dove on my plate than rhino and
elephant." Then he say he try for canvasback duck the next day.
Esau answer that the game may be small but, if it is good to eat, it is
worth huntin'.

When Marse John Henry git home, his mother was a-sittin' on
the porch. She git up and come down the step to meet him.

Young Missus Harriott face always be scrub to shinin' clean-
liness, a-glowin' with health, and she look younger than her year.
'Cordin' to old pictures, her eyas show intelligence 'neath thick

lash. Her hair, brushed and glis'nin', was pull back tight in a thick bun on the crown of her head. Durin' the day she wear a stiff starch apron and, as simple as it was, it enhance her clean good look.

As always, Marse John Henry kiss his mother warmly and she tell him what a sweet boy he is. He musta known he was the very light of her life.

About that time Marse Fred, Marse John Henry father, come out and tell him that the next day a visitor was a-comin' to Hampton Plantation. Marse John Henry want to know who it is. Marse Fred say the man was from up No'th, and they call him Paul D. Marse John Henry mother declare she gone write down ev'ry detail of that visit. And that she did, for sure.

Marse Paul D arrive soon after breakfast the next day, and he was all dress up in a tweed suit and vest. The horses was ready for the hunt when the guest arrive.

The men set out for the place where they could bring down a quantity of duck. Marse John Henry had his gun and was 'spectin' to have the time of his life watchin' Marse Paul D. As it turn out, Marse Paul D was quite clumsy, 'though he could hold forth on subjects from politics to the pullin' of teeth.

When the first cloud of duck be scare up, all the Hampton men hold back and allow Marse Paul D to have the best shot. Missus, that Marse Paul D be full of the right intention but wrong conception. He done such poor shootin' he not bring down a single duck. That annoy Marse John Henry so much he decide then and there he will not hold back anymore. Iffen that rich New Yo'ker cannot shoot any better than that, he don't deserve to fill his bag. When the next cloud of duck be scare up, Marse John Henry fire. That boy bring down so many Marse Paul D surrender his gun to Marse John Henry.

But that not be the end of that story. Them men next go out in a boat. Marse Paul D stand up and try to shoot a duck and he fall into the cold river. When they pull him back into the boat, his face and hands was a-turnin' blue. The men rub his hands and face and warm him up.

When the huntin' party 'rive back home, Marse John Henry mother and gran'mother be there a-waitin' on the porch and he run and kiss them. They ask him what the bag was, and he say they had bag some duck. What kind? the women want to know. Marse John Henry say they git some canvasback and mallards, and then he say quite serious, "We also got a blueblood." They look at him funnylike and ask what he mean by that. Without hesitatin', he say that Marse Paul D take a tumble into the river.

When a Cat Bites a Snake

One thing for sure, Missus, Marse John Henry mother and gran'mother give that boy all the love he ever dream of. While she was a-carryin' that child, young Missus Harriott often speak of the love she would 'stend to that little person, who would be her own flesh and blood. She have plenty of opportunity for that.

And Missus Harriott, the gran'mother, love him ev'ry bit as much. And she seem to have more time to spend alone with him than his mother did.

One day Marse John Henry and his gran'mother decide to go out ridin'. A groom be sent to bring their horses to the porch of the mansion. As they wait, Marse John Henry gran'mother play 'round with her white cat, which she call Missus Tartleberry. She hold that cat up to her cheek and love her. When the horses 'rive, Missus Harriott put the cat down on the porch.

Marse John Henry mount his horse, and the groom help Missus Harriott git on hers. Missus Harriott was a-leadin' the way out of the yard when suddenly her horse shy. Then it rear up. That startle Marse John Henry, 'cause he want nothin' to happen to his gran'mother. He jump off his horse and see a big diamondback rattler a-lyin' just where the horse had shy. His gran'mother turn her horse in another direction and ride over to a big tree.

Missus Harriott sit in the saddle as she watch her gran'son go to a tree and find a limb what been blown down by the wind. He take that limb and hit the snake on the head. Marse John Henry say he gone take that dead snake to the wood and 'spose of him, but his gran'mother say no, to wait 'til they return from the ride. The dead snake was a-lyin' in the yard near the Washington Oak, and it would prob'ly not be notice 'til they return.

So, off they go, a-gallopin' with the wind in their face. They fly down the road to the Pretty Wood and then slow make their way through the trees and brush.

Later on, 'fore they go back home, they stop and git off the horse and sit on a grassy knoll and talk a spell. Marse John Henry just love to have his gran'mother for hisself like that. He ask her to tell him somethin' 'bout her childhood. She say she tell him 'bout the time she meet the Princess of Wales in London.

When Missus Harriott was little, her fam'ly take a trip to England. Before they leave on their trip, her mother, Missus Eliza, and her father, Marse Charles Pinckney, talk 'bout presentin' Missus Harriott to royalty. Missus Eliza tell her daughter she should take a gift to the royalty, somethin' native to South Carolina. Missus Harriott think on that, and she decide to take three Carolina bird. She select a indigo bird, a nonpareil, and a yellow bird. The plantation carpenters make three elaborate cage for them bird, and the cage resemble them French country houses. The Pinckney take them bird all the way over the ocean to England.

When the fam'ly git to England, they learn King George II was on the sunset side of his reign, and Marse Charles and Missus Eliza choose to take Missus Harriott to visit Princess Augusta at Kew, where she have set up a court of her own. She was the Princess of Wales, and her son would be the next king of England. But gittin' a invite to meet with the Princess of Wales was no easy task.

Marse Charles git hold of a man they call the Gent, and he

speak to the Princess household servant. The Gent was told the Princess see no person she do not know, for fear someone ask a favor of the Crown. The Gent attest to the credit of the Pinckney. He say Marse Charles is one of His Majesty Council of South Carolina and want nothin' but to show his affection for His Majesty and all his royal house. When the Gent return to the Pinckney quarter, he say Princess Augusta will see the fam'ly at eleven o'clock any day the followin' week.

The next week Marse Charles, Missus Eliza, and Missus Harriott, a-holdin' her bird cage, pick a day and ride in a coach to Kew. When they call at the palace, they was told the Princess had gone a-airin'. Now, Missus, is that principle and manners? I don't think they had much of that in England. But Missus Eliza be a thinkin' woman, and she quick write a note what say somethin' like this: Missus Harriott Pinckney, daughter of Charles Pinckney, Esquire, one of His Majesty Council of South Carolina, pay her duty to Her Highness and humbly beg leave to present her with a indigo bird, a nonpareil, and a yellow bird, what she did bring from Carolina for Her Highness.

Finally, someone from the palace come out to the coach and say for the Pinckney to come again the next day. If they not choose to do that, the servant say, they can leave the birds.

The Pinckney return to their quarter, and that night they receive a message that the Princess of Wales be glad to see Missus Pinckney at one o'clock the next day.

The next day Marse Charles, Missus Eliza, and Missus Harriott dress in the finest quality clothes what Chas'n have to offer and head for the palace. They was receive by a old lady who say the Princess was a-dressin'. After 'while a man come into the room and ask the three visitor to follow him. They walk through four grand rooms to the Princess dressin' room. Princess Augusta hurry to meet them at the door.

Little Missus Harriott present the birds and say they is typical of birds at her home in South Carolina. The Princess of Wales say she was 'fraid one of them be a favorite of hers, as one zackly like it appear in a portrait on her wall.

They was all seated, and the Princess ask 'bout the weather in South Carolina, and if they have a good governor. She say the king always was please to hear his province have good governor. Marse Charles tell her he fear they have intrude upon Her Highness and he think they should withdraw, but she tell them not to go. 'Bout that time Missus Harriott feel tired and flurried and happy at the same time and she begin to cry. The Princess of Wales call Missus Harriott her "little angel" and ask her to come and sit on her knee. Then the Princess call for her own children to come close, and Missus Harriott git to meet all of them.

In the room they was in, was collections of good old English chinas. The Princess go to a cabinet and take out a figurine. She hand it to Missus Harriott and tell her it is a gift.

That was the most 'straordinary visit with the Princess of Wales, and any American would agree with that.

Marse Charles keep his family in England five year and then he decide to come back to South Carolina. Missus Harriott return with her parents, but her brothers, Marse Tomm and Marse Charles Cotesworth, stay in England for their schoolin'.

After Missus Harriott finish tellin' her story, Marse John Henry kiss her on the cheek and thank her. He say he never forgit her tellin' him 'bout that trip to England and her visit with the Princess of Wales.

Missus Eliza and Missus Harriott talk all their life 'bout that trip to England, and how little bitty Missus Harriott present them bird to the Princess of Wales.

Marse John Henry and Missus Harriott not come home from their ride the same way they go, but come back through the meadow and push them horse to the peak of their endurance. I hear tell that the ears perk up and the tails stand out and they fair fly in the wind.

When the two riders 'rive home, the groom meet them and take the rein. Marse John Henry commence a-lookin' for that snake, as he wanta make good riddance of it. But he could not find it. His gran'mother help him look and they go all 'round the yard, and they search under the trees and 'mongst the shrubbery. They cannot find the snake.

Finally, Missus Harriott tell her gran'son he likely had not kill the snake, and it come back to its sense and make escape. Marse John Henry not wanta accept that for the answer, but finally he agree his gran'mother must be right.

Missus Harriott start up the steps, and she gasp and back down a step or two. Marse John Henry look at her, and he see a 'spression on her face he never seen before. He ask her what is wrong, and she say for him to look at Missus Tartleberry.

Marse John Henry look at the cat, a-sittin' on the very top step. The rattles on the end of the snake tail was a-hangin' out of the cat mouth. Missus Harriott scream that Missus Tartleberry had eat the snake. Marse John Henry never see anything like that in his entire life, and he ask his gran'mother what they can do. She say she cannot bear to lose Missus Tartleberry, and they would take her to a *healer* on the plantation and see if there was any herbs or some sort of treatment for the problem.

Missus Harriott call for the groom to bring back the horse, and as he had not yet take off the saddle, they be soon on their way to see Madam Tallulah. Missus Harriott hold Missus Tartleberry in her arms, with the rattles a-hangin' from the cat mouth, and Marse John Henry ride to the rear.

They come to a cabin by the river, and Madam Tallulah open the door. She be dress in a robe of white cambric, and from elbow to wrist run bracelet of silver and other metal. The chink of anklets come from her ankle bones.

You see, Missus, people give that healer all kind of gift for her treatment. It was irregular treatment, I can tell you that, but the old people believe in her. Yas sirree. They believe in her altogether. Even Missus Harriott go to her in that emergency.

Madam Tallulah wear a white turban 'round her head. That cloth been wound 'round many time, with not a wrinkle to be seen. It be pristine clean. In my mind eye I see her a-washin' that turban ev'ry mornin', ironin' it careful so as not a ridge or furrow show.

Missus Harriott ask Madam Tallulah iffen she have anything to give the cat. Madam Tallulah take the cat and look at it, then pass it back to Missus Harriott. The woman say she have some roots what might give Missus Tartleberry some energy, but she not believe they should do anything but leave her alone. Madam Truth say in a few day they not see any of them rattles. I don't recollect if she say what would happen to them.

Missus Harriott and Marse John Henry ride back to the plantation, and Missus Harriott fix a nice cool place for Missus Tartleberry 'neath the porch. Missus Harriott advise her gran'son not to go 'round the cat for a few day.

Missus Harriott hug Marse John Henry and tell him she sorry their ride had to end that way. Then she lead her gran'son to her room and she open up that big old armoire. From the bottom drawer she take out a bureau scarf what she make with her own hand. She unwrap that scarf and lift out a exquisite figurine. It was a woman a-standin' on a hill, and the wind was blowin' her skirt. Missus Harriott hand that figurine to Marse John Henry. She tell him that the Princess of Wales give her that figurine, and she want him to have it as his very own. Marse John Henry kiss his gran'mother cheek, and he take that figurine to his room at the top of the stairway and place it on the bureau.

The next mornin' Marse John Henry was thinkin' 'bout what adventure he might find that day. He walk out on the porch and look 'round for Esau, but he not see him. Instead he see Missus Tartleberry. The rattles from the snake she had eat was gone—and they was never seen again.

The Murdering Swine

All the Rutledge fam'ly be sittin' at dinner one afternoon and they was a-laughin' and talkin' 'bout their favorite things. While they was enjoyin' that meal, at 'bout three o'clock, all of a sudden the sheep in the pasture let out a pathetic bleat. Marse John Henry ask what that was. His father who been a-listenin' to ev'ry word by his sons, say he did not know. He look at his wife and his mother-in-law, but they shake their head. All the fam'ly git up and go onto the porch. Just then Esau run up and say a wild hog drive the sheep in the pasture into a cluster under a oak tree. He say the sheep was actin' silly. The sheep was a-actin' plum idiotic, he go on to say. Somebody in the fam'ly say the sheep not be very bright under the best of circumstance.

Marse John Henry take off toward the pasture, and Esau be right behind. Marse John Henry father and brother follow, and the father call out that old hogs is 'specially dangerous. Marse John Henry and Esau was to take no chance or try to be a hero, he say.

To tell you the truth, Missus, Marse John Henry was a-givin' Esau a lecture of his own. He was sayin' that razorbacks was the most dangerous animal in the wood. They have tusk what come out just above the upper teeth, and a razorback could tear up a man in seconds.

Just then the men come on the scene. The cause of the trouble was not a razorback but a old sow, half-wild. Esau say he know 'bout her, and she be the mother of 'leven little pig. Esau say he know who own the old sow. It was a man who never take care of his animal. This hog starvin' half to death and had turn killer, he say.

The sheep was cluster under the trees, lookin' on as the sow devour a lamb. It was all such a unusual pageant ever'one just stand stock-still a'tryin' to take it in. The men suddenly notice a old ewe, a-standin' 'tween them and the sow. She just stand there, a-watchin', helpless. What a feelin' she musta had, seein' that little lamb go like that!

All of a sudden, Marse John Henry run into the wood. He come out with a live oak limb and advance toward the old hog. Marse Fred cry out for his son to stop, hollerin' that he not know what danger he is in for. Then Esau call to Marse John Henry, tellin' him to withdraw and let nature make its own rule in that contest. Marse John Henry brothers was a-wringin' their hands. Marse Fred call out again, sayin' the sow is evil and not 'fraid of the devil, and Marse John Henry oughta back off and leave well enough alone.

By now Marse John Henry have a solid hold on a limb, and he march right on in for the attack. The sheep killer look up and see him a-comin'. Marse John Henry father and brothers be yellin' at him to stop. Esau have his say 'bout that and tell his friend he goin' to his death in the jaw of that sow. But Marse John Henry march right on. Just before he reach the spot where she stand, the old hog turn to the sheep under the tree and charge. When she come out on the other side of the herd, she have another lamb in her jaw. They tell me she dart through the wood ev'ry bit as graceful as a deer, jumpin' over the low bushes, a-holdin' the lamb high.

Marse John Henry git madder than ever. His feet suddenly take wing and he set off after the old sow. Then he git a plan in his head, and he turn and go another way. He run 'round in a circle and in a few second come out ahead of her. Now they was eye to eye— the ole sow still a-holdin' on to that lamb.

Marse John Henry father yell that the old sow was famish, havin' fed 'leven little piglet, and she was so hungry she done gone mad. She would eat anything in sight, he say, even Marse John Henry! But the boy not have a fear in this world. He seem to be gone mad too and he was shoutin' as he fly up to that sow and bring that limb down on her snout. She turn and take off, lightin' out for a different part of the wood, still a-carryin' the lamb. Marse John Henry be right in behind her.

She stop at a openin' in the forest and drop the lamb. Marse

John Henry dash up and hit her again with the limb. She loosen up on that lamb and he grab it and start back into the wood. He look back a time or two, but she not be a-comin' after him. He say she was still smartin' from the blow.

Marse John Henry brother Marse Fred take the lamb and carry him. As the men walk back to the house, they talk 'bout that old sow and how mad she was. Marse John Henry father say she had taste blood, and they must watch out for the sheep a few days.

That little lamb be give a good bed under the porch of the mansion, and after that Marse John Henry and his father and brothers go back into the house and finish their meal.

After gobblin' their last bites, they go back into the yard. Esau was waitin' for his friend. Marse John Henry father ask Esau if he know who the old sow belong to, and Esau tell him it is a man who live in a shack by the river. That man, 'cordin' to Esau, was a ne'er-do-well, and what little he had come from fish he catch and sell. He not feed his hog, and she turn sour.

Marse John Henry father tell Esau he like for him to lead the way to the man cabin, so he can take a look at the situation. But before they go there, he believe they should go once more to the sheep in the pasture. This time they go prepared. Marse John Henry have a gun on his shoulder.

Just as Marse Fred predict, the old sow had return for another meal, and the sheep was cluster under the tree again. Marse John Henry raise his gun, but his father call out to him to take the gun down.

"But that old sow is eatin' our flock," Marse John Henry protest.

Marse Fred have another idea, he say. He tell his other sons to herd the sheep into the stableyard. At the same time, Marse Fred and Marse John Henry and Esau run the sow away.

It took the rest of that day to git them sheep to the stableyard. After the little lamb had improve, it was move there too.

One day durin' them three week the sheep stay shut up, Esau lead the way to the shack by the river. Marse John Henry father be distress at the condition of that shack and the man who live there. He tell that man if he not do right by his hog he will run him offen the place. And he tell that man iffen he not have anything to feed his old sow he can come to the mansion any day and they give him scraps and enough food to keep the animal from starvin'.

The old man say he sure be glad they not kill his sow, and he will find her and take better care of her. He thank them over and over again for savin' the sow life as the little piglets need her bad. And while he be in such a good mood he ask them men iffen they know that a young girl upriver done gone into a trance. That be somethin' what happen now and then in that day and time.

The men all take off to that girl cabin, and Esau and Marse John Henry be glad of that. They want to see that girl. When someone fall into a trance, that was the spout, bark, rant, and rave of the plantation. The people what believe in conjure could scare them Rutledge children pretty good, but Marse John Henry feel safe that day 'cause his father was with him.

When the group arrive at the girl house, she done out of the trance. A look of relief spread 'cross the face of Marse John Henry, and his father tell that girl not to believe in that sort of thing. He 'splain to her that a spell cast by a conjurer could cause a person to become ill and slowly waste away 'til he be dead. In that day and time people have strong belief in such as that.

That girl say she been born with a cowl, or veil, over her face. If you been born with a cowl over your face, you have strange power to foretell the future, to see thing that is lost, and such as that. Many people been born with a cowl over their face, and they say they have second sight.

I don't believe in conjure. I live here by the grace of the good God, but them old people way back yonder believe in it. Yas, Missus, them Rutledge children delight in hearin' all 'bout that conjure stuff.

Wildcat Fight

As Marse John Henry grow, he begin to enjoy fishin' so much he decide to make that his life work. His fam'ly tell him he must become a planter, and when he have his own plantation he can hunt and fish to his heart desire. He did not take to that old philosophy and for awhile he was near'bout a solitary fisherman. Some of the time Esau go with him. Most time he go alone.

Marse John Henry mother had seven other head of children. While he not be better than the others, Marse John Henry was sure different. His mother note the difference early on. Mighta been 'cause he was an unexpect child. I always hear tell they be somehow different. The old story go that Marse John Henry just appear on the scene one day. That old story also say his mother look into his eyas and git some sort of message. She say she could never quite figure it out, but she know he would be her special child. That was 'spose to be their secret, but others talk about it.

Marse John Henry involve hisself in constant activity, what prob'ly had both bad and good aspect. He would sometime disappear for hours, without anyone knowledge where he was. Then he would reappear like a ghost.

Marse John Henry was a loner and he sometime feel he was strange and not at all like his brothers and sisters. He say he be in tune with the whistlin' willet and the great wood ibis and the curlew a-callin' 'cross the marsh more than he was with people.

He always take good care of his canoe, cast net, and gill seine. And he have a great assortment of line, hook, and sinker. He make friends with other fishermen, learn his way 'bout the meanderin' creek, inlet, lagoon, and waterway. While at the dinner table, if the conversation ever come to Sandy Point, Eagle Hammock, Five Fathom Creek, Bull Island, or Cape Romain, he know all 'bout them place. He also know all 'bout the animal what live in them place. 'Casionally he would see a wildcat, and that was a subject what bring on much discussion. He also talk 'bout the marsh wren, otter, 'coon, and 'gator.

Sometime Marse John Henry go to the river or one of the inlets at night. In the stillness, he hear the scream of battle, and usually he can tell who the fighters be. Iffen a 'coon run afoul of a wildcat, most folk believe the contest to be one way. But the 'coon be in his own element 'round water and Marse John Henry come to believe that iffen a 'coon git in a fight near a inlet, he stand a chance of winnin' the battle.

One day at dinner, Marse John Henry say he know 'bout a fight 'tween a wildcat and a 'coon, and the 'coon be the winner. His three brother take exception to that. 'Though his mother usually take his side in thing, she not have much to say 'bout that. Like the others, she have trouble believin' that any sort of animal could win a battle with a wildcat.

The day what follow that one, Marse John Henry father suggest that perhaps the boy been mistaken. He point out that a wildcat is a vicious animal, large and strong—they prowl at night and can win 'most any fight. He name several books in the Hampton library what have to do with wildcat. He suggest his son also look up lynx and bobcat in them books.

Marse John Henry know his fam'ly not believe him. They never would come to term with a wildcat losin' a battle to a 'coon. One day while he was walkin' on the riverbank, he seen the carcass of a wildcat a-lyin' on some dry sedge. The body was torn, and it had for sure been in battle. A flat bank of mud 'stended to the water, and pawprints in that mud show the fighters been the wildcat and the 'coon.

The next day at dinner, Marse John Henry tell that story, and it seem no one believe him at all. His father just shake his head and his brothers snicker. But Marse John Henry mother take up for him, and she say she believe it with all her heart. 'Course, there was no way in the world to prove it, 'cause the tide had come and went two time since the fight, and all pawprint done been gone by that time.

Marse Fred, Marse John Henry father, git up from the table. He stretch his shoulders and say he feel like a walk. Anyone want to go? he ask. 'Course Marse John Henry say yas and he know Esau would wanta go. Marse John Henry brother Marse Thomas Pinckney say he have a new dog what be a pointer and he would like to take him and see if he is a true sportin' dog. So, they light out, Marse Fred sayin' he like to go to the place where the 'coon done kill the wildcat.

Marse Tomm name his dog Sport, on account of he was in the category of sportin' dog. His father comment that the dog seem to be sensible and show some trainin'. He ask his son iffen he been a-trainin' the dog and Marse Tomm answer that he had. The animal, Marse Fred say, was shapin' up as a fine huntin' dog.

As the men walk along, the dog, what had a brown head and white mouth, go a-lookin' for somethin' to point out to the men. Ev'ry now and then he stop, lift his right front leg, and stand froze with his tail stickin' out straight. "He got somethin'," Marse Tomm say. Then the dog start a-runnin' again and he go on for awhile. Then he stop, make his stance, and look with all the eyas he got. He be as still as a statue. A bird would fly up, and then he go on a-lookin' for somethin' else to point at.

After a hour or two, the men come to the place where Marse John Henry say he saw the prints. That wildcat body was gone!

Marse John Henry just scream out that the carcass of a wildcat had been on the sedge. But as hard as he look he couldn't see it.

"Uh-huh," his brother say, a-soundin' like he thought Marse John Henry done gone and told a lie.

"Let's don't jump to conclusion," the father say.

Marse John Henry look as hard as he could, a-tryin' to find that carcass, but it was nowhere in sight. He even git Sport on the trail, and he tell that dog to find that carcass and point at it. But the dog just run 'round on the muddy bank. Even Sport be indifferent to the story of the wildcat.

"Where is the dead wildcat?" Marse John Henry brother ask. "You say he was here."

Marse Fred say 'most anything coulda happen to it, but his voice not have much conviction.

Sport had a white tail, but 'bout two inch from the end it was brown to the end. That dog git into the water and begin to splash 'round, and you could see that brown knob of a tail goin' up and down in the water. He was not a long-hair dog, like a setter, but he git soakin' wet.

Marse Fred and the boys sit down on a grassy knoll and talk 'bout the dog as they watch him. Marse Tomm say he be so proud of Sport. A cousin, one of the Pinckney of Fairfield Plantation, give Marse Tomm the dog and it was clear he consider it a valuable gift.

"I believe you can teach that dog to be a fine huntin' companion," Marse Fred say.

Esau was sittin' by Marse John Henry. "They not believe what you say 'bout the wildcat," he whisper. Marse John Henry just drop his head. Afterwhile, Marse Fred say it is time to go back home.

Marse Tomm and Marse Fred agree they not see anything what give a clue to a wildcat or a 'coon. Marse John Henry say to Esau they ain't never gone believe him now. He was gone try and forgit all 'bout that fight. 'Cause he wasn't never gone convince anyone in his fam'ly that a 'coon could kill a wildcat or any other large animal. Esau agree, and he tell Marse John Henry there be plenty of other adventure they can enjoy.

At that very moment, Sport give a yelp.

Marse Tomm call out that Sport is in trouble.

Oh-h-h-h-h-h, talk about trouble! First, that dog head out of the water, and then not. Then the brown knob tail above the water, then gone.

"What is goin' on here?" the father yell.

They all say it at the same time, as clear as anything. A big old 'coon was on top of that dog.

Blood now trickle through the water, and Marse Tomm jump into the creek. But, the dog even snap at him. His father call for him to back away. He say that dog was tryin' to defend his life, and he could turn on his master under them circumstance.

Marse John Henry call out that the 'coon was in his home environment in that water, and the dog was not. That 'coon had the upper hand, he say, and he add, "just like he did when he fight the wildcat."

Ever'body look on, helpless. The 'coon was winnin' the fight, and there was no question 'bout that. More blood fill the water. Then the raccoon be on top and the dog be under the surface of the water.

"That 'coon done won that fight," Esau say.

Ever'one agree the raccoon won that fight—as well as the fight with the wildcat.

And you know what, Missus? Marse Tomm finally git his poor sportin' dog out of the water and start a-carryin' him for to bury, when he see somethin' under a tamarisk bush. He take the toe of his boot and push it out. And right there be the carcass of the wildcat, for all to see.

Marse John Henry done won that fight the same as the 'coon.

The Wild Boars

Another story, Missus, what Marse John Henry mother write in her journal be 'bout them old wild boar. Them Hampton women sure know how to write the story of Hampton!

On a mornin' when there was no real need for food for the plantation table, Marse John Henry done git up 'fore first light. He decide to take a walk toward the river. Oh, how he love that mighty Santee River! And he love the wilderness of that lonely delta. He even love that old mean swamp what be infest with 'gator. Sometime he just like to watch the sun rise over that place.

As he mosey 'long on that particular mornin', like always, he be cautious in case he see a deer or wild turkey. Right 'fore he reach the river, a-standin' on a bluff above the water, he spy a movement. There was just enough light for him to see, but not too clear. Suddenly two huge forms come into view. They was wild boar, what he believe just cross the river, and they start rootin' up a heavy mulch of oak leaves. They not see or hear Marse John Henry and he turn and light out for the house to git his gun.

When Marse John Henry return to the scene, them brutes still be a-rootin' up ever'thing in sight. Them boars be destructive, on account of their size and natural meanness.

Marse John Henry took aim and shot. Just as the gun go off, the boy lose his balance and fall into a ditch. As he go down, he see one of them brutes a-headin' for him, runnin' like a wild hyena. Marse John Henry scramble to his feet and he see both them wild hyenas a-comin' for him. He musta thought they was gone have him for breakfast. He pull off two shots as fast as he could. He have no idea where them shots land, as he just shoot at random. The sun was not yet up, so his sight was still short.

Marse John Henry struck out for the wood, a-thinkin' 'bout them boar and the damage they could do to him 'cause of their size. When he turn to face them, they was still on his trail, gittin' closer all the time. He stop quick and send three shot in their direction. Then he commence to run again. When Marse John Henry turn back to look, both them boar lay dead. He estimate that be 'bout seven hundred pound of pork a-lyin' on the ground.

Marse John Henry not go home. He go straight for Esau house. When he tell Esau that he done shot two huge boar and his fam'ly can have them, Esau call his parent and they summon some of their friend. Great rejoicin' take place right then. Later, after the wild hog was butcher, Esau fam'ly try to give Marse John Henry a big ham, but he refuse to take it as his fam'ly did not need it.

The Ghost Bells

Marse John Henry Rutledge like nothin' better durin' the years
he be a-growin' up than goin' over to the old church of Saint Jame
Santee. The old brick church be just a couple mile from the Hampton house, and it be in a quiet settin', what Marse John Henry say
remind him of all them old people who been gone to Glory. Some
of them people been lay to rest right there, Missus. Right there in
the churchyard of St. Jame Santee lay the remains of a Horry and a
Rutledge and many other who been gone to their reward a long
time now.

The old church be somethin' to see. It was the fourth one in
the parish, build in 1768. I can't forgot who was on the buildin'
committee, for me old Missus make me remember that. There was
Marse Thomas Lynch, who sign the Declaration of Independence,
Marse Daniel Horry, Marse John Drake, Marse Jacob Motte, Marse
Paul Mazyck, Marse Elias Horry, and Marse Jonah Collins.

When that buildin' was design, it was plan to hold two con-
gregation—the French Huguenot and them from the Church of England. To satisfy both them group, the church was build with two
portico—one a-facin' the road for the English and the other facin'
the French quarter. Front and rear portico was support by four brick
column. After some time pass by, that rear portico was wall in. Durin'
the time Marse John Henry be a-growin' up, eighteen fam'ly was
on the parish church roll and the reverend priest been Marse William Mitchell.

That church in the beautiful wildwood near Wambaw Creek
be a place where Marse John Henry love to spend some quiet time.
One day as he was sittin' there on the steps a-thinkin' 'bout the
gone-on ones, he hear a church bell. But as he think about that, he
know it was not a church bell. No one was at the church on that day
as it was not a day for divine service. He listen good, and he think
he hear that bell a-ringin' again.

St. James Santee

Marse John Henry decide he gonna sit there 'til he come to a conclusion 'bout the bells. If there was ghost bells at St. Jame Santee 'Piscopal Church, he wanta know who that ghost was. And as he think about that, he resolve it could be 'bout anybody. So many of the gone-on ones could be a-comin' back as ghost.

Just then, he hear the ringin' again, and he think to hisself it sound like harp music in the wind comin' from the crest of the tall yellow pines off to his left. He look over toward the pines and he disover it was not harp music at all. A rattlesnake was a-lyin' in the path what lead up to the church steps. He was a-ringin' his *bells* to beat the band. And then Marse John Henry hear the sound of rattles a-comin' from over on his right. There 'mongst the wild azalea lay another rattler, and that one too was a-ringin' its bells.

Marse John Henry not believe them snakes even see him. It was early November—the end of the matin' season—and he believe with all his heart them snakes was communicatin' with one another. So Marse John Henry commence to think on that.

While he was a-studyin' 'bout them snakes communicatin',

he witness another spectacle. You know what, Missus? A squirrel come up that path, and that little animal not see the snake. He come mighty close to the reptile, what was smart and take notice of him.

That rattlesnake turn his 'tention from the snake he was a-courtin' to try and snare a meal of that squirrel. The squirrel stop and scratch in the soil.

The old rattler seem to know just what to do to git that meal. Even though that squirrel now move into strikin' distance of the snake, the snake not make his strike. No. He go into his coil, inflate hisself to look big, and at the same time sound his bells. Just then the squirrel see that snake, but the poor squirrel be render power-less to do anything. That snake look like sudden death, when just a moment before it was a-lyin' there communicatin' with another snake only a few feet away.

Marse John Henry continue to watch. That little squirrel couldn't move a hair. Oh, that snake put on a show for him! And all the while the squirrel be too scared to breathe. The snake had com-pletely charm that little squirrel. Then the snake make his move, and that squirrel be dinner for the snake that day.

Marse John Henry done had enough of all that. The story goes that he not wait 'round to see if the courtin' continue. Them bells what he think was the old church bells a-ringin' turn out to be two rattlesnake a-courtin'. And 'though them rattler could go on to kill one of the cows, dog, horse, or even, perhaps, finish off Marse John Henry hisself, he just leave them right there. After all, he had seen a rattlesnake charm other animals before. He say he had witness that many time, when a rattler render a rabbit, bird, cat, and chicken helpless by charmin' them.

Missus, that be what Hampton Plantation was like in that day and time, and that be why Marse John Henry love it so much. He be a-livin' in the deep wood, where a boy could git firsthand all them lessons of nature. He set out to learn all he could of nature, 'cause that be what he love so much. His mother and gran'mother could talk to him hour on end 'bout a-marryin' the daughter of a rich planter, but what he love was the wood. In that day and time, he never believe any woman can top that.

The Gun Clubs

Horse racin' was a business, but huntin' was a sport.

Rutledge men always be interest in racin'. They git the well-bred runnin' horse and mare from England, and ev'ry year them mare drop one or more colt. No part of America 'cept Virginia produce so many fine horse for the course, saddle, or draft as South Carolina. Some plantations have what they call the Chickesaw breed. They be introduce by the Spaniards into Florida, and in the course of time had increase to astonish. They was handsome, but they be small, not more'n thirteen and a half hand in height.

At Hampton Plantation, the mare be cross with English blood, and they produce colts of great beauty, stren'th, and swiftness. All that racin' be held down in Chas'n.

Huntin' be carry on by clubs what have their first begin in the day of Marse Charles Pinckney, Missus Harriott father. Hunt clubs spring up ever'where by the time Missus Harriott gran's be a-growin' up at Hampton. A gun club exist in ev'ry district of the Low Country. Up in Waccamaw there be gun clubs, and down in McClellanville there be the Santee Gun Club. There be plenty of people who tell you that them men way back yonder spend their happiest hours at their gun club.

They meet early in the day with their hound, horse, and gun. Such as choose to take a active part in the sport sally out to the rear of their dogs. As soon as a deer is spied, the hound commence the chase in full cry. Missus, them woods out there echo with sounds more exhilarate than any music instrument.

Them men know the plantation and the habit of the deer and

what course the deer take. The men gallop through the wood with a haste what sometime 'ceed that of the dog and deer. Oh, them Rutledge men be hunters. Oh, man!

Marse John Henry Rutledge, the next to the last head of children of Marse Fred and Missus Harriott, take a different stand, but one ahead of the game. As soon as that deer appear within gun shot, he level at it. He be a near'bout perfect marksman. A deer hardly ever 'scape and was generally lay low by his first or second shot.

When the hunt end, the party return to the clubhouse with keen appetite and partake of the dinner what been supply for them from the wood. The rest of the day was spend social. In the evenin' the hunters divide the spoil and go home.

When the Rutledge men grow old and the Lord come a-callin' for them, the sons keep up the tradition of the hunt. South Carolina gun clubs be immortal.

And, Missus, when good service be need by the country—you know, such as in military service—them Low Country men know marksmanship like no other men. They be ready for war.

Women back then not take to huntin' but they offer a table of wild game to satisfy the palate of King Solomon. The wild turkey, venison, or duck, what come from the wood, git prepare in the outside-the-house kitchen and carry to the big house. In the big house, Missus Harriott make ready. She take the fine white Irish linen tablecloth from the sideboard drawer and throw it over the great round table. She arrange place settin's of silver and run back to the sideboard for the dishes. She take the good chinas, the old Nankin, East India, or Crown Derby, and she set the table, leavin' space for the large silver trays of meat what the men bring down in the wood. And the Madeira what be serve was not rainwater. *No-o-o-o.*

There be plenty of wild game serve in them Chas'n mansion too and guests be often invite to the meals. There was always a man of science or an artist what the Rutledge invite to the dinner table. Marse John Henry take a interest in the game serve at them meals.

Marse John Henry like to shoot at Harrietta Plantation too, with that big old house still a-sittin' over there on the river empty. But he love huntin' on Hampton best of all.

Perpendicular Burial

There happen 'bout that time, Missus, somethin' so peculiar, even though it happen at Peachtree Plantation what be situate 'tween Hampton and Harrietta, I think I ought to tell you 'bout it.

Peachtree Plantation been a beautiful place. One time it belong to the Lynch fam'ly. You know, Missus, old Marse Thomas Lynch sign that Declaration of Independence. Later on, Peachtree go to the Motte fam'ly. But it always be own by blueblood.

The marse of Peachtree have a beautiful daughter, and he be right fond of her. One day she was a-standin' on the plantation dock when a ship come in from the sea. The marse run down to the dock to see who was a-stoppin' there.

The captain of that ship say, "Mon Capitane, we dare not keep this man on board. He is at death door with scarlet fever." The captain push a sick man toward the marse of the plantation and say the ship will come back for him in a few day, after he recover.

The marse say the sick man cannot be treat at Peachtree, and he cannot accept him for he would spread 'round that contagious disease.

The young girl scream, " 'Course we take him."

The father say, "No!"

And then the girl recite some stripture what say, "He that have pity 'pon the poor lend unto the Lord; and that what he have give will he pay him again."

The father relent and motion for the boatmen to bring the sick man ashore. The girl stoop down and take one of the man's hand and say somethin' what soothe him. The father scream for her not to touch the man, but she already done that. The father tell the girl to go and fetch two slave. As the girl take her leave, the ship slip away from the dock.

The slave, Cudjo and Bonaparte, come and, as they move the man, the father say his daughter was always 'ceptible to illness. He tell the slaves to keep the man as far from his daughter as they can. Then he watch the ship move down the river.

The next day the sick man pass on. The ship did not return to pick him up, and the marse of Peachtree bury the body on the far side of the plantation.

Ten day later, the daughter come down with signs of scarlet fever. Her father git 'bout wild with anger. He send for three physic. Both the girl mother and father be sick with worry.

Word spread of the girl illness. People at Hampton hear 'bout it and some of the worker in the Harrietta field also. Three day after them symptom show up the girl go to Glory.

The other planter folk here'bout drape their carriage in black and go to Peachtree to grieve with the fam'ly. The father despair and would not see them. That poor man 'bout slap crazy in pain.

He tell his fam'ly he cannot bear to see his daughter bury in the ground a-lyin' down. He finally put the girl body in a pine coffin, what Cudjo and Bonaparte had make. He carry the coffin hisself to a place overlookin' the South Santee River. He tell Cudjo and Bonaparte to start a-diggin' earth what be use to cover the coffin. They begin to dig a hole in the ground, and he say, "No!" He tell them he will hold the coffin upright and they is to cover it with earth. That go on near'bout all day, and finally that coffin git cover. The daughter be in the coffin, and she be a-standin' up.

The father go to that site ever'day to visit the standin'-up coffin. He plant hackberry and sugarberry plants over the mound of dirt . Holly form a outer circle and b'yond that was a circle of camellia. Missus, iffen you wanta see that mound, I take you there. 'Course it be almost camouflage now by brush and trees what lap overhead. But Sue can show it to you, right over yonder at Peachtree Plantation. And I show you the ruin of the Peachtree house. The ruin of that big old brick house be right elaborate.

Time Clarifies

Missus, the test of courage is not to die but to live. I know 'bout that. Sue been there. Now goin' on my second hundred. But time stretch it long arm and clarify all thing, and on the twelfth day of April, 1821, Marse Frederick Rutledge die, leavin' young Missus Harriott a widow. That woman they believe never marry be a widow. They was way off 'bout her. 'Though her husband gone to Glory, she did not throw his name in the discard. He was bury in the church-yard of St. Michael Church in Chas'n. Great was the lament over that loss. Up yonder in Glory, God mortar and pestle be a-sortin' the rice from the hull.

Once more, only ones livin' at Hampton Plantation is women and children. Missus Harriott Pinckney Horry still be the head of the plantation. Her son what live in Paris stay over there, and he claim no hold on the place, 'though he was the rightful owner. Missus Harriott brother Marse Tomm keep in touch with her and send letter by anyone comin' to Hampton. In one letter he scold her for not writin' to him when she know her gran'son Marse Fred was goin' to Chas'n. He say, "I just return from the office and I met Frederick Rutledge in town. Oh, Harriott! How could you let such a opportunity 'scape? Not a single line nor even a message."

There not be many time what Missus Harriott let slip by and not write a letter. She was a woman on her feet. Oh, how shrewd she was when she was shrewd, but always to the good of her friends and fam'ly.

Marse Tomm help Missus Harriott all he could. He write to her in March of 1822 and advise her to use as many hand as need be

to keep the rice field at Harrietta in order. That plantation house
been still empty, but they work the land. And Marse Tomm remind
her to keep the fields at Hampton in crop, as well as them in the
delta 'tween the North Santee and the South Santee Rivers, and on
the island near the mansion. He tell her to find two good plows to
be work by ox. The ox will trench plow the whole of the plantin'
land through the summer, he say, and this will revive the soil for the
next crop. His letters give her good instruction.

Missus Harriott do all he say and she be please to have his
remindin' what regard the plantin' of the field. Marse Tomm prob'ly
believe it be the hardest thing for a woman to be a rice planter and a
society woman at the same time. But Missus Harriott could stand
up to ever'thing.

There be plenty of young Pinckney and Rutledge to fill the
plantation with happiness, and they did that, sure 'nough. Hampton
Plantation be the biggest place anywhere here'bout. 'Course it was
in the country, but it was so big it be a town all to itself.

All them who sprung from Missus Harriott have manners and
principle, and they put that to use. They blueblood, but they not
uppity. Their good trainin' 'specially show when they attend the St.
Cecilia. You know 'bout the St. Cecilia, Missus?

You see, the St. Cecilia Society quit with the concert and start
up with the balls, what be very grand. I can't forgot what me old
Missus tell me 'bout the St. Cecilia. Little of what she tell me 'scape
these ear and eyas. Oh, my sight not be so good now, but these eyas
be large, keen, and brown when me old Missus speak, and my ear
been perpetu'ly cock.

The Rutledge and Pinckney women attend the balls at St.
Andrews Hall, a handsome buildin' in Broad Street. The Society
own its plate, damask, chinas, and glass, and a good stock of Madeira. The suppers, fix up extra, been wait on by ev'ry butler and
footman in town who could git a swallow-tail coat. Any one of them
butlers grin with delight when he 'dentify his acquaintance, 'spe-

cially *his own fam'ly.*

Oh, Missus, that be a grand time for the Rutledge and Pinckney women. Balls and horse races and banquets and fashion and ever'thing. No war too close behind or in front, and rice be a-bringin' in the most money of any crop ever to be known in this country. That time was sure the closest thing to King Solomon time there ever was. King Solomon, the son of King David and Bathsheba, the woman King David fall in love with and marry, have ever'thing in abundance. And people just keep a-bring him more. The Queen of Sheba visit him at his palace in Jerusalem, and she give him gifts of rare spice, precious stone, and 120 talent of gold worth near four million dollar. King Solomon have ever'thing.

And the rice planter have all of that too. What more could they have? I have thought 'bout that, and I don't know what it can be. And they 'sociate with the highest in the land.

Partridges and Paroquets

Missus, iffen you had count all the head of children of all the missus of the coastal plantations, you see that few women raise all them children to maturity. That be because of the fevers. There be three fevers rage, but the most deadly was malaria. And all the white people on the plantation been expose to it, as that germ be bred by a mosquito what hold forth in the low-lyin' rice field. The sick months was August and September, and in them month thousands gone over the Jordan long 'fore their time.

If a body down with the country fever, or what be a bilious fever, and a doctor was send for, ever'thing was made ready for the visit. Bandages and a basin was place 'side the bed for the bloodlettin', and calomel was sure to follow. If luck favor the sick, the fever git run out of the system. After that, a tonic of Peruvian bark was pour down the victim, and he could avoid a summer funeral. When winter set in along with dropsy and pleurisy, the victim wish he had gone on to the grave. The worst thing 'bout all that, the planters not even know a mosquito in the rice field been the cause of the fever.

Time come when the planter leave the plantation and stay gone from frost to frost. After the last frost of the season, the fam'ly head to the ocean or the mountain. Some take the grand tour of Europe. Others go to the springs in Virginia for what they call "the cure." When the planters come back in the fall, first question always, "Who died?"

The mountains of North Carolina lure the Hampton people, and young Marse Frederick buy some land at Flat Rock. Missus Harriott gran'son not be natural planter. No, sirree. Marse Edward wile his hours away talkin' 'bout the Navy. And Marse Fred actin' all biggity 'bout his mountain land.

Flat Rock was different from the Low Country as the day is from the night. The Up Country have high mountains and deep valleys, and trees be of the species of hemlock and others what not be natural to the Low Country. And the weather up there stay cool all summer. When Marse Fred come back to Hampton after the first frost of the fall, he say so many people from the Low Country be at Flat Rock they call it "Little Chas'n."

The slave people not be 'ceptible to malaria fever due to their particular sickle cell, and they stay right here and take care of the rice field. The children play little games. One be call "Put a plate o' rice here!" They git in a circle, and one child stand in the middle. While he try to 'scape, the others go 'round and 'round and chant, "Put a plate of rice here! Eat all o' that? Put a bowl of peas here! Eat all o' that?" Then the one in the circle say, "Marse bring the barn down! I can't git out of here!" He sing that four time, then he sing, "I lost the barn key. I'll hunt 'til I find it." And they repeat all of that and have a jolly time.

Missus, I don't hear tell of any of the rice planter livin' on their plantation durin' the summer month 'til quinine come to be, and then there be some good treatment for malaria fever. But them graveyard in all them woods you see out there, all the way from here down to Chas'n and up to Georgetown, and even all the way down to Savannah, be full of children and missus and marse what lose their life to that fever. You can see that on the markers. The servant and field hand just live on and lose their life in their old age or by accident or they git wash away durin' a hurricane.

All the people who plant on the South Santee River go back and forth to Chas'n near'bout all the time. But you know, Missus, there be a tavern where they stop for food and drink—Hallwell Tavern. That be on the bank of the South Santee River. And there be a ferry there call Mazyck Ferry. After all the people from Georgetown, on their way to Chas'n, cross over on Mazyck Ferry, they stop at Hallwell Tavern for to rest up awhile. The Hampton folk not have to cross on the ferry, but they go to Hallwell Tavern anyway. That tavern serve food and drink but they specialize in quail, or partridge as they call it at Hallwell Tavern. But the Hampton men git plenty of that at home.

All them young Rutledge men go near'bout crazy over huntin' partridge. Partridge be good, 'most as good as duck. And the field be full of covey of partridge.

The men put on their huntin' clothes and take their gun and dog and leave early in the mornin'. The cook be ready for them when they git home. The cook clean the partridge and fry them crispy in a huge black iron skillet. Then they make a little brown gravy for the biscuits. Oh, man, ever'body by the name of Rutledge love to go partridge huntin'.

And back in that day and time there be huge flock of bright green paroquets on the South Santee River. I never see that with these old eyas, but me old Missus tell me 'bout them. Ever'body who see them say they be the brightest green. Nobody ever shoot a paroquet that I hear tell of, so I don't know what happen to them.

Well, Missus, let me tell you about somethin' astonish what happen with them Hampton folk. You ready? Marse Edward Cotesworth Rutledge up and marry Rebecca Motte Lowndes, and, Glory be, they decide to live at Harrietta Plantation. Can you believe that, Missus? Finally, that manor house was to have someone a-livin' in it. It was a spooky place, never havin' been live in, and at the same time it was kept planted and was love by all member of the Rutledge and Pinckney fam'ly. The bride and groom gather up the furniture and portrait what Missus Harriott had envisage for that house and the young couple fix it to suit their taste. They move in and ever'body be jubilous! All the talk was 'bout Harrietta Plantation a-havin' a marse and missus.

Then, lo and behold, Marse Edward decide to enter the Navy and, when he leave for that duty, Missus Rebecca move out of Harrietta. That fine old house sit there empty again.

While Marse Edward Cotesworth away in the Navy, his wife, Missus Becky, drop their first child: a daughter name Harriott Horry. They call her Harrie. Missus Harrie be the light of their life, as well as that of her great-gran'mother, Missus Harriott. Missus Becky and Missus Harrie spend a lot of their time at Hampton and they go to Harrietta often. 'Though nobody live at Harrietta, it be a special house to them.

Marse Frederick and his wife, Missus Henrietta, also be at Hampton when they not at their home in Flat Rock. They have a daughter call Lize. The children gran'mother write to her son in the Navy and say how much she wish he could see the little girls a-playin' together. She say that Missus Lize call her little cousin "Harrot Horry," and the gran's call her their "little perfection." There was lots of talk 'bout them gran'daughters—who they would marry and their education.

The best school in that day and time for young women was Madame Talvande school in Chas'n. Oh, Missus, let me tell you 'bout that astonishin' woman.

Madame Talvande know more 'bout manners than anybody who ever live in Chas'n. I hear tell 'bout a heap of women who go to her school. She mighty nigh teach manners and principle to the whole country 'round about. You could pick out any woman who attend Madame Talvande school. They have the best manners.

Madame Rose arrive in Chas'n in 1793, after she 'scape a slave uprisin' in Santo Domingo what leave many white planter people dead. The Santo Domingons settle down in Chas'n, and their center be in Archdale Street. Two of the women was very beautiful: Madame Margot and Madame Rose. Madame Rose marry Marse Andre Talvande, and they buy the lot on Legare Street.

The first owner of that lot be the Solomon Legare fam'ly. Marse Andre and Madame Rose build their house in 1819, and the house what be there now be call "The Sword Gate House." The Talvandes never become American citizen, but Madame Rose know how to teach music, dancin', French, and manners best of all. All the young planter fam'ly women go to that Chas'n school.

Madame Talvande believe dancin' skill is important and she teach her student dance lesson, for which their father was charge $34 per quarter. Madame not be lenient with her student. While little Missus Harriott attend that school, she write her father 'bout it. Let me see iffen I can recollect them French words she say— "The Chas'n *jeune fille*, educate at one of the schools, learn beside her lesson a careful demeanor and a absolute su'mission to her teacher." Them words would astonish the young people of this day and time. But Madame Rose Talvande git them young women ready to traffic with the high-ups in the world.

All the young and old alike be ready in April 1825 for the triumphal arrival of the Marquis de Lafayette. He come to see what the city be like, the same as the Queen of Sheba who go to see King Solomon riches. And you know who stand right up there to greet Marse Lafayette? It sure 'nough be General Thomas Pinckney and General Charles Cotesworth Pinckney, Missus Harriott brothers, in

full regimental dress for the 'casion. After that greetin', Marse
Charles Cotesworth deliver the address of welcome.

But, Missus, time clarify ever'thing, and that welcome to Marse
Lafayette be the last public appearance for Marse Charles Cotesworth
Pinckney. He die in August of 1825, and three year later Marse
Tomm die in Chas'n. That same year, 1828, Marse Charles Lucas
Pinckney Horry of Paris die and Hampton Plantation go to Missus
Harriott.

And that not be all who go to Glory that year. Missus Elizabeth Pinckney Rutledge, the third child of Marse Fred and Missus
Harriott and the gran'daughter of Missus Harriott, die while still in
her twenty. That be a sad time, sure 'nough.

Now Missus Harriott own Hampton Plantation outright. You
'member, Missus, how her husband, Marse Daniel, leave it to their
son, 'cordin' to that old law of first born? But after Marse Daniel
take the son to England for his education, the boy never return to
America to take over the plantation. At the son death, Hampton go
to the mother.

With both her brother gone to Glory, Missus Harriott now man-
age on her own. 'Course her daughter, young Missus Harriott, help
her, and her gran' Marse Frederick also. And Missus Harriott be the
best at takin' care of all her workin' people. That be why ever'body
want to be Rutledge people.

One day, Missus Harriott hear tell of a small child who was a-
standin' in her fam'ly cabin when a wild boar enter by the door. The
child was a-holdin' a piece of bread in her hand. Snatchin' at the
bread, the hog tusk catch the child hand near the thumb. When a-
runnin' off, the hog carry the child with it, draggin' her along into
the field. All the other children and some men run after the hog and
catch it. Missus Harriott go and git that child. She take her into the
mansion and git a doctor to come treat the hand. After that, Missus
Harriott 'tend the child herself 'til the little girl be perfectly heal.

Missus Harriott was a workin' woman. She plant that rice at

Hampton and Harrietta, entertain, and keep up that Chas'n house. But she remain close to her gran', a-seein' that they go to all the horseraces and balls and have a education. And she was 'specially close to her gran' Marse John Henry. There be no confusion 'tween them.

Marse John Henry, like all the other Rutledge children, start to grow up. He cast a eye toward a woman to become his wife, and his gaze fall on the daughter of a pharmacist. He fall hard for her.

Now you know, Missus, how Marse John Henry mother and gran'mother talk to him 'bout selectin' a woman from the planter stock. Well, when Marse John Henry gran'mother hear 'bout the daughter of a pharmacist, she fix herself up with a good dose of determination. Her life was give way entire to lecturin' to him. She say that 'though the young lady may possess rare beauty and charm and be the pride of her mother and father, the planters would not regard her. She go on to say a woman who begin in that trade, even though her father may have put some of his money in land, never become a proper mistress of a plantation.

Marse John Henry mother point out how all the Horry and Rutledge and Pinckney wife be planter stock, and them fam'ly had never been water down by any pharmacist stock. They count them out. Marse Edward Cotesworth, Marse John Henry brother, had take Missus Rebecca Motte Lowndes for a wife, they remind him. She was a gran'daughter of Marse Thomas Pinckney, Missus Harriott brother.

Marse John Henry brother Marse Fred had marry Missus Henrietta Middleton Rutledge, his cousin from Nashville, Tennessee. She was gran'daughter of the great Henry Middleton who start Middleton Gardens in Chas'n, and daughter of Arthur Middleton who been president of the Colonial Convention. And that be just a sample of the marriage, all what been attach to the quality. Ever'one had marry well, 'specially Daniel Horry in Paris who marry a niece of Marse Lafayette. And then Marse John Henry desire to marry the daughter of a pharmacist! That would not be tolerate.

Marse John Henry was outrage! He say he want to marry someone he could love to the end of his days. He had not found a woman
like that 'mongst the *quality*.

The whole fam'ly git jiggle up tight with anxiety, and when
force was threaten, Marse John Henry bid defiance. That boy face
take on a forbiddin' quality what make his gran'mother shift in her
seat.

Missus Harriott and Marse John Henry mother decide to lay
off a day or two. But they fret when he start a-spendin' most of his
time a-rockin' in a chair upstair in his room. He not go huntin' and
fishin'. No sirree.

But they not relent. They not want a bad ear of rice in that
fam'ly. Up to that time all the head of children been name after
their ancestor, and the name been 'most the same in several genera-
tion. They not want any new name add to that list.

Again the women tell Marse John Henry, "No!" He fume and
fuss up in his room, still a-rockin' in the same chair. The women
decide silence be the best treatment, and they ignore Marse John
Henry. Durin' that time, the women be a-searchin' their brain for
the likeness of a suitable woman for him.

One day Marse John Henry come downstair and say he goin'
away for a short visit. His mother and gran'mother be jubilous, as
they think he might be gittin' over his love for the pharmacist daughter. They have some up and down 'bout the dead and decease Missus
Eliza and how she still carry on under such troublous circumstance,
and they come out loud a-singin' her favorite hymn, "When all Thy
mercies, O my God, My risin' soul surveys." And they count on
Marse John Henry emotional sufferin' not a-goin' into physical pain
and mortal disease. Oh, Missus, that be a day of strong resignation,
what time and trouble never shake.

Marse John Henry go to the office of the pharmacist. The
daughter not know he gone there. Marse John Henry explain all. He

say his mother and gran'mother not accept the pharmacist daughter as his wife. He say that he, Marse John Henry, be so anxious he cannot leave his room. The pharmacist tell him he cannot treat a broke heart. Then the pharmacist tell him he never allow his daughter to marry into such a fam'ly as that. Iffen his daughter marry Marse John Henry, she be a outcast, someone of no consequence. The other women in the Rutledge fam'ly look down on her even more than their servant.

Marse John Henry know for sure all is lost.

The fifth day of March, 1830, come 'round, and Marse John Henry spend that day in his room, a-rockin' in the chair. The women in the house listen to that *rock . . . rock . . . rock.* And then the rockin' stop. Suddenly, there come a blast from a shotgun.

The women run upstair and there was Marse John Henry a-slump over, and a pool of blood be on the floor.

His mother scream, stoop down, and hold his head in her two hand. She say, "Don't die. I would a-rather have you marry to anyone than have you dead and decease."

His gran'mother be a-ringin' her hands. She git down on her knee and try to hold her daughter and her gran'son. They cry and fret and say any woman be better than a suicide.

Oh, Missus, that fam'ly been brought to it knees. All the other planter fam'ly come, carriages drape in black, and they try to console the two Missus Harriott. But, there be no consolation at Hampton house.

These ole eyas never seen them, but I hear tell letters was flyin' 'round that fam'ly 'bout Marse John Henry killin' hisself over that pharmacist daughter. That be a brokenheart time.

People what kill themself not be allow in the fam'ly burial plot. Marse John Henry be bury near the door on the river side of Hampton, and you can see that marker today, Missus.

In Memory of John Henry Rutledge, Son of Frederick
and Harriott Horry Rutledge, who departed this life
on the 5th of March 1830 aged 21 years. He was distin-
guished for Fortutude & firmness. The Goodness & the
magnanimity that he showed even in the agonies of a
painful Death made indelible impressions upon all who
witnessed it. He died in Peace with all men & in the
full Confidence that his Maker would receive his Soul
with that Mercy & forgiveness which is the hope & so-
lace of the Penitent in his approach to the throne of
the Eternal.

I hear tell that Marse John Henry live long enough after the
shot ring out to repent to God for his sin, includin' takin' his own
life.

Now, listen to this, Missus. Several week after the burial, some
servant hear that chair a-rockin' up there in Marse John Henry room.
They know nobody be up there, but they go up and look and that
chair be a-rockin'. And they do their best to scrub up that blood
offen the floor, but the blood bubble right back up. And the chair
keep a-rockin'.

There be much up and down 'bout Marse John Henry ghost.
Some say he open windows what be close, and he shut windows
what be open. He light up candles and snuff out them what been a-
burnin'. I can tell you this, Missus, and this is sure 'nough the truth.
I, Sue, and my son Will Alston both scrub that floor many a time to
remove that bloodstain, but it just bubble right back up again. And
that chair keep a-rockin' 'til it was carry away from Hampton Plantation.

Missus Harriott, the gran'mother of Marse John Henry, never
lose sight of her good fortune, even in troublous time. She write in
'bout all her letters, *Sincere is my gratitude to heaven for the advantage of this period of life, as well as for them that done pass.*

Oh, Missus, it bring a tear to my old eyas to think back on Missus Harriott. The last year of her life not be rig up in advantage. The Lord come a-callin' for that sweet woman in December, 1830, nine month after Marse John Henry gone to Glory. She be eighty-two year old.

For upwards of half a century, Missus Harriott been powerful concern 'bout her children and gran'children marryin' into the planter class. What done happen with Marse John Henry sure 'nough a shock in this world. That poor woman die of a broke heart.

When Missus Harriott pass over, it be the saddest time. I know when she enter the pearly gate, Saint Peter be a-standin' there. And there be a host of angel to greet her, all in white flowin' robe and with white wing.

Missus Harriott Horry Rutledge, daughter of Missus Harriott, now the owner of Hampton Plantation. That woman whose own mother believe would never marry and be the mistress of a plantation now be the mistress of Hampton, and of Harrietta Plantation still a-sittin' over yonder empty. Of Missus Harriott and Marse Fred eight head of children, only six be a-livin' at that time.

Marse John Henry been lay to *anything but rest* out there by the back door. People who come to Hampton house say they can feel his presence. I don't know 'bout that, but I can still see where that blood a-bubble up on the floor. And I can still hear the voice of me old missus, Margaret Hamilton Seabrook Rutledge, as she sit on the porch of Hampton house a-tellin' me all the old story. That I can't forgot.

Epilogue

Now, Missus, ever'thing 'bout today style is brand new to me. I tell you the truth. I like both the style, the old style and the new brand, but give me my old style.

I don't care how anybody judge the world, but I think this is a good world to live in, if you understand. I had a good time. But when I think 'bout Hampton in the old days . . . . Oh, Lord, iffen only I could go back to that Hampton house like it was in the old days and look in just one more time, just one more time.

Missus, I'm gone pray for you tonight. I'm gone pray from the bottom part of my heart. When I see someone who wanta hear my voice tell 'bout the old-style Hampton, I feel rich.

Thank you, Missus.

*Nancy Rhyne interviews
Sue Alston at her home in
the 1970s.*

Nancy Rhyne interviews
Sue Alston's son Will on
the steps of the Hampton
Plantation mansion,
in the 1970s.

Nancy Rhyne and Will Alston

Sue Alston and her son Prince

Bibliography

Alston, Prince. Interviews by author. Hampton Plantation, McClellanville, SC, early 1970s.

Alston, Sue. Interviews by author. Hampton Plantation, McClellanville, SC, early 1970s.

Alston, Will. Interviews by author. Hampton Plantation, McClellanville, SC, early 1970s.

Fitzpatrick, John C., ed.. *The Diaries of George Washington: 1748–1799, Vol. IV*. Boston and New York: Houghton Mifflin Co., 1925.

Georgia Writers' Project. *Drums and Shadows*. Athens, GA: University of Georgia Press, 1986.

Grimshawe, Leming. *The Church of St. John in the Wilderness, 1836–1936*. Pamphlet, 1968.

"Hampton Property Purchased by State," *Charleston News & Courier*, November 23, 1971.

Horry, Daniel. Will, proved before Charles Lining, esquire, November 18, 1785. Will Book A 1783–86, 572. Clerk of Court, Charleston, SC.

Joyner, Charles. *Remember Me: Slave Life in Coastal Georgia*. Atlanta: Georgia Humanities Council, Georgia History and Culture Series, 1989.

Pinckney, Elise, ed.. *The Letterbook of Eliza Lucas Pinckney: 1739–1762*. Chapel Hill: University of North Carolina Press, 1972.

Ravenel, Mrs. St. Julien. *Charleston, The Place and the People*. New York: Macmillan, 1929.

Rutledge, Archibald. *Home by the River*. New York: The Bobbs-Merrill Co., 1941.

_____. Papers, 1860–1970. South Caroliniana Library, Columbia, SC.

Rutledge, Irvine Hart (son of Archibald). Letters to and telephone interviews by author. Hagerstown, MD. Varied dates, 1978–1994.

_____. *Tales of Hampton*. Hagerstown, MD: Self-published, 1987.

_____. *We Called Him Flintlock*. Columbia: R. L. Bryan Co., 1974.

Smith, Alice R. Huger, and D. E. Smith. *The Dwelling Houses of Charleston, South Carolina*. New York: Diadem Books, 1917.

South Carolina Department of Parks, Recreation and Tourism. *Brief Chronology of Hampton Plantation*, Columbia, SC: South Carolina Department of Parks, Recreation and Tourism, undated.

The South Carolina Jockey Club. Charleston, SC: Russell & Jones, 1857.

Stoney, Samuel Gaillard. *Plantations of the Carolina Low Country*. Edited by Albert Simons and Samuel Lapham, Jr. New York: Dover, 1989 (1938).

Wheeler, Mary Bray, and Genon Hickerson Neblett. *Hidden Glory: The Life and Times of Hampton Plantation: Legend of the South Santee*. Nashville: Rutledge Hill Press, 1983.

Webber, Mabel L. "Dr. John Rutledge and His Descendants." *The South Carolina Historical and Genealogical Magazine*, Vol. XXXI, no. 1, January, 1930, 93–106.

Wilkinson, Margaret. *Horse Racing in South Carolina*. Interview by C. S. Murray. December 29, 1939. On file at Library of Congress, Washington, D.C.

Williams, Frances Leigh. *Plantation Patriot, A Biography of Eliza Lucas Pinckney*. New York: Harcourt, Brace & World, 1967.

Note from the Author:

My work for this book depended heavily upon the narratives of the Federal Writers' Project in the 1930s, on file at the South Caroliniana Library in Columbia, South Carolina, and the Library of Congress in Washington, D.C. My interviews in the 1970s with Will and Prince Alston, sons of Sue Alston, also figure prominently in the story. My work with the Alston family when writing articles published in *South Carolina Magazine* in the 1970s was of great help in the formation of this narrative.

About the Author:

Author and storyteller NANCY RHYNE lives in Myrtle Beach, South Carolina, with her husband Sid, who provided the photographs for this volume. Nancy is something of a local celebrity and a much-sought-after speaker across the state. She has a keen interest in southern folklore and spends much of the year gathering new material.

Nancy Rhyne's other books include

Alice Flagg: The Ghost of the Hermitage
Carolina Seashells
Chronicles of the South Carolina Sea Islands
Coastal Ghosts
The Jack-o'-Lantern Ghost
Low Country Voices
More Tales of the South Carolina Low Country
Murder in the Carolinas
Once Upon a Time on a Plantation
Plantation Tales
Slave Ghost Stories
The South Carolina Lizard Man
Southern Recipes & Legends
Tales of the South Carolina Low Country
Touring the Coastal Georgia Backroads
Touring the Coastal South Carolina Backroads
Voices of Carolina Slave Children

Sue Alston on the porch of her cabin

Hampton Plantation is now a park managed by the state of South Carolina. The mansion still stands and is open to the public for viewing.